I CAN STILL DO IT!

The Unstoppable Spirit
of a Plane Crash Survivor

Karen Trolan

Robert D. Reed Publishers

Robert D. Reed Publishers • Bandon, OR

Robert D. Reed Publishers
P.O. Box 1992
Bandon, OR 97411
Phone: 541-347-9882; Fax: -9883
E-mail: 4bobreed@msn.com
Website: www.rdrpublishers.com

AUTHOR WEBSITE: www.ICanStillDoIt.com

Editors: Victoria Cooper and Cleone Reed
Cover and Book Designer: Cleone Reed
Photo Credits: Crash Photo of firefighters, Sierra Sun, Truckee, CA
    Legends of Martial Arts with Grandmaster Rothrock, J.F. Belle
    Work Photo, Brandon Barnett

ISBN 13: 978-1-944297-28-2
ISBN 10: 1-944297-29-9
Library of Congress Control Number: 2018930585

Designed and Formatted in the United States of America

Dedication

To my husband Steve Trolan,
whose sincere love and encouragement
helped me recover and adapt,
making all my amazing activities possible.

And to my children
Lindsay, Andrew, and TJ
who were positive, gracious, and supportive
with our family's change in life.

"Success is to be measured
not so much by the position
that one has reached in life
as by the obstacles
which he has overcome."

~ Booker T. Washington

Acknowledgements

Thank you to all the people who made a difference for me in my "new" life:

Steve Trolan for all his love, support, and encouragement.

TJ, Andrew, and Lindsay for all their understanding, help, and love during recovery and life.

Herb and Beverly Weinman, my parents, for raising me with a strong can-do attitude and staying positive as well as being my advocate in the hospitals. Also, thank you for adding ramps and a lift/elevator in your home.

My brother, Curtis Weinman, for driving from Utah to be at the hospital to support me. He was the only one there when I came out of surgery.

Holly Vargas, Valerie Westbrook, and Diane Rudy for their consistent encouragement and exceptional support throughout.

Sharon Kelleher for visiting me in the hospital to give me expectations of the injury, and continued to role model paraplegia abilities, helping me to laugh at situations like falling out of my chair at work and on the soccer field.

Jon Cohan and Bav Thakrar for coaching the competitive soccer team while I was in the hospital and then encouraging me to continue coaching.

Dave Heckley, Realtor, a friend with the same level injury, for helping me understand what to expect, challenges and solutions. For always being positive and encouraging: you are a great role model for a Realtor.

Dr. Zhu and Dr. James Lu for their tireless efforts working with me to rehabilitate and stay strong.

Niki Lamb for her encouragement to horseback ride and get me out on the trails, showing me how.

Landa Keirstead for teaching me how to ride and working with my horse on how to respond to my riding with me.

Susan Henderson for giving me a sweet, well-trained horse that I learned to ride, even on trails.

Kathleen O'Neill convincing me to ride a Tennessee Walker, teaching me how, and then getting me out on trails and camping too.

Shihanke Russ Rhodes for adapting martial arts to work for me in the wheelchair, and for the years of training previous to the accident which set up the new art.

Alex Franckx for being my martial art training partner and helping adapt techniques to work from the chair.

Jeff Barnett for creating a position for me managing in real estate and encouraging me to go into leadership with Silicon Valley Association of Realtors and California Association Realtors.

Paul Cardus for supporting me through leadership and all types of real estate meetings and conferences for Silicon Valley Association of Realtors, California Association of Realtors (C.A.R.), and National Association of Realtors (NAR).

Dr. Marc Stoner for giving me a broader outlook, recommending me for the Hall of Fame, helping me with pain management and healing, and introducing me to wonderful martial artists and training in martial arts.

Grandmaster Mark Gerry for working with me to expand and better my Martial Arts and helping me to continue to enjoy life.

Grandmaster Samuel Kwok, "the miracle man," for teaching me Wing Chun basics and healing with amazing acupressure.

Master Bob Hodge for training Steve and me in self-defense arts.

Vince Arthur for providing amazing support for the entire family initially and throughout rehab.

Forrest Philpot for encouraging me to be the candidate trainer and working with me to do ski patrol.

Brian Volpe, Ed MacBeth, and John Lincoln for helping to install ramps in my home and being there for me.

Chaplin Sipantzi for powerful prayer and compassion while I was in the hospital and constant follow-up.

Thanks to everyone who offered their help and who these stories are about. Thank you for touching my life and to God for your miracles!

Table of Contents

Foreword

My wife, Karen Trolan, has dealt with challenges all her life. And, she has always been able to focus on her end goal and succeed. To do this it has taken lots of hard work on her part. This book is her sharing the challenges she has overcome following a horrific experience that occurred in 2009: a plane crash which broke her body in many ways and left her without the use of her legs. I, too, was in that plane but only suffered multiple compressed vertebrae in my lower back.

This book could have many titles: *Adapt and Overcome, Attitude is Everything, Out of the Darkness,* or *I Don't Do Can't.* Ultimately, *I CAN STILL DO IT!* was the culmination of discussions with many friends who, over the course of several years, expressed these sentiments when describing Karen. Many people asked her to write a book because she had accomplished so much following the accident.

Karen was not happy with creating a semblance of her life before the crash. She wanted to continue to live life to its fullest. You will read in these chapters about the challenges that she has learned to master through perseverance with a great attitude—simple things that she had to learn to do for daily living to more advanced activities like skiing, horseback riding, and martial arts that required hours of practice, overcoming failure, and injury. Although the stories in the book are many, do not fool yourself into thinking that it happened overnight and was easy for her.

I understand what hard work and sacrifice look like. Having served in the U.S. Army Special Forces as an officer, the regimen we undertook to stay in shape and hone our skill has always served to remind me that failure is a learning experience that forces us to improve. Quitting was never an option. Although Karen never served in the Military, her drive is similar to that of the soldiers with whom I served.

From the time we met, over 36 years ago, she never liked to sit around and watch. When we lived in Hawaii, I was a bagpiper with the Honolulu Pipes and Drums. She would come down to the practice with me; but instead of watching us practice, she learned how to play the tenor drum. Within a couple months she was performing with us, never letting time go to waste.

As life with her progressed, we always kept busy. Even though we had our different careers, our time together was always active, whether running, cycling, SCUBA Diving, or whatever outdoor opportunity came our way. When I used to get injured, Karen used to say, "You were just having fun." So, after the plane crash, I told her "You were just having fun!" Now as life progresses and she adapts her life to paraplegic activities, we remember that we are *just having fun* and never allowing ourselves to focus on the negative but moving forward with a positive attitude.

This book explores the challenges that Karen has gone through, the physical and mental challenges that she faced, and still faces, and her refusal to be a held back by what society expects from her condition. Anyone with challenges, whether physical or mental, will find a message of strength and resilience in her words. Life is too short to pity yourself for whatever event has befallen you. Everyone has challenges put before them in life. Some are obvious to others; some are not.

Karen's story will hopefully inspire all who read her words. It should not only inspire those who need help but also inspire those who can reach out to those in need. Karen's accomplishments could never be achieved alone. She has grown through the support of old friends as well as many new ones she has met on this journey. What was important is that she made the effort to get out there! Once there, the miracles occurred and the resources and contacts continued to appear in our life.

As NASA says, "Failure Is Not an Option;" neither is it for Karen. Enjoy her story and be inspired to make your own.

~ Steve Trolan

Introduction

Pilots rarely survive small-plane crashes. I was piloting my family's Cessna out of the Truckee airport near Lake Tahoe, California, on Labor Day Weekend nine years ago when the plane crashed. In an instant, my life changed. I became a paraplegic. "I Can Still Do It" is a quote that I find myself saying all the time, and with my long road to recovery, I am constantly surprised not only that I survived but what I can still do.

This book is my personal account of how I have had to be courageous and full of determination to navigate through the multiple injuries in my brain, neck, lung, spine, ribs, and a number of bones, requiring months of hospitalization and years of rehabilitation. Enduring a feeling of helplessness that comes from being wheelchair-bound, my family and I found ways to come together and knitted together a plan not just to live but to thrive.

Buttressed by my Christian faith and my husband's dedicated support, we dealt with the worst trauma of my life and its antidote—the creation of regimens of physical therapy, medical treatments, adaptive sports, and travel—to recapture the joys of my earlier life.

One of my big concerns was that all the "firsts" that I had pre-accident would not lend themselves to new firsts. But instead, I have been blessed with so many new opportunities, with new firsts and meeting the most amazing people. And, many things that I had accomplished in the past laid the groundwork for me to build upon as I maneuvered through my "new life."

"Opportunities don't happen:
you create them."
~ Chris Grosser

My journey has been referred to as "one of pushing through adversity." I credit my upbringing to parents who instilled a "can do" mentality in my brother and me to always have a positive attitude, regardless of what life dishes out. I also believe that because I have always been athletic, that contributed to my discipline and desire to return to the sports I so loved: snow and water skiing, horseback riding, swimming, kayaking, and ATVing. Today, I still love all of these and do some adaptively, with the help of my husband, who muscles me into kayaks, skis, gondola lifts, and onto the backs of horses.

The ability to give back to others by helping and teaching also inspires me to work hard every day on my core strength. I am very grateful that I was able to return to every one of the teaching and mentoring roles in the work world and my volunteer activities before the crash. By inviting me back to the Ski Patrol at Northstar, the Disaster Aid Response Team in Los Gatos, and Girls on the Run (GOTR), as well as to my coaching activities with my kids' sports, those organizations helped me to feel myself again; and given the opportunity to work part time allowed me to get back on track quickly.

Originally, I was encouraged by friends, colleagues and caregivers to write a book about what I was going through. As the book took shape, I kept to the truth to help others become aware that we all have difficulties in our lives; it is how we respond and deal with the situations that show our character plus make us better, stronger people.

My wish for you as you read about my journey is to find the silver lining in your own story. Work hard, fight hard for every success and achievement. Every accomplishment has value no matter the size. It is important for all of us to be appreciative for what we have and all we can do every day. And it is most important to give ourselves credit for all the ways we have been courageous in our lives, for everything we have accomplished, and for all the things we have gone through and come out victorious.

Although this is a story about me, it really is a story about you, your friend, neighbor, or loved one. My hope is that you will understand how you can be supportive to them and if it is you, how you can push through any adversity! I found that "I can still do it" and so can you!

Chapter 1
The Plane Crash

When our six-seater Cessna crashed in Truckee, California, we beat the odds and survived.

Remains of our plane

September 7, 2009 passed the same way that many of our summer days at my parents' vacation home did in North Lake Tahoe, California. My husband, Steve, and I had taken our daughter, Lindsay, and one of her girlfriends along for a weekend in the mountains. Lake Tahoe was one of our favorite getaways, since it offered recreation and relaxation year-round. We were a family of sports enthusiasts and packed a lot into each day.

I especially liked piloting our small plane, a 1964 Cessna 206, to Truckee because it combined the challenge and beauty of flying into and out of the Sierras. Although I had previously flown into and out of the

Truckee general aviation airport several times that weekend, the winds could change within moments, so I checked and rechecked the weather forecasts. For every flight, I would compare a computer-generated plan with a manual one that I prepared. Because of the winds and the density altitude of this mountain airport, I double-checked everything. After weighing all of our baggage and us, I worked out the weight and balance as well as other details. Now, my flight plan was ready to be called in to flight services to check the weather again and get updates on NOTAMS (a Notice to Airmen is a notice filed with an aviation authority to alert aircraft pilots of potential hazards along a flight route or at a location that could affect the safety of the flight), so that I would have all the research and information that I would need for a successful flight. This flight plan was checked several times during the day, to make sure that it was a go for a takeoff at around 6:30 pm on this early autumn evening.

The girls finally woke up (typical teenagers) and we ate breakfast. Once breakfast was finished, we had to focus on cleaning the house. My parents allowed us to use their great Tahoe cabin, as long as we fully cleaned the place when we were done. We each divided up the duties and jumped into our own responsibilities.

The house was cleaned, the car returned, the bags all loaded in the plane, giving us enough time that we took a pit stop at the airport. I went upstairs to the "non-dispatch tower." There I was able to discuss the winds, departure, and other important items with another pilot. The runway had the wind running down the runway with a slight crosswind. The weather looked good for a take-off.

Because my pre-flight check took time, the girls sat under the plane's wing in the shade. I checked the plane inside and out, checking everything, including all that was on my checklist. Since it was my plane, I took extra care to make sure it was right! My check included calling the Unicom (airport information) again, since it changed every hour. It was close to the hour, but it hadn't changed again yet.

As usual, after a thorough pre-flight check, the engine started nicely and I taxied to the run-up area after a radio call (at the non-towered airport). I could see and hear that no one was in the air or on the ground at the time. I had hoped that at this early evening hour someone might be able to give me some feedback about the air just above the airport, because none of the reports I read or was told about showed any information about it. So, I had to rely on the airport report, which was almost an hour old, and I looked at the windsock. Both those indicators showed a "go."

Revving the engine was always a good check, showing that it should work well in the air. It sounded great, and the gauges read as they should, so I taxied over to the runway, staying at the very start of it in order to give me the longest distance for takeoff. I kept the brakes on and revved the engine. When the torque was good, I let go of the brakes and accelerated down the runway. When I reached the point where the speed was fast enough, I rotated (pulled the yoke back and started to climb). In high-density altitude in the mountains, I had to go faster and stay longer on the ground in order to have enough airspeed to make a good climb.

Everything was working perfectly as I took off. The plane started climbing nicely, and I continued adjusting the controls as necessary. I was out of ground effect, and the plane continued to climb. Our cockpit was silent: My passengers knew to be quiet so I could listen to the radio and the plane.

We were about 500 feet above the ground which was halfway to the pattern altitude. I was just about to start a crosswind turn (a left turn), making the second part of the rectangle for departure, but the plane jolted and the nose popped up. "What's going on?" I thought. I did what I was trained to do—fly straight and drop the nose of the plane to pick up speed—which would give us lift. Even though the plane picked up speed, I felt like it was being pushed down.

Things happened so fast from that point on. We hadn't lost much altitude as I brought the nose down and the speed up, but then the right wing dropped. Something was wrong, and I was determined to do my best to keep the plane in the air and flying. While I leveled the wings, I tried to stay calm. No one said a word in the plane, and neither did I. I had trained for all types of emergencies, but I had never felt like being in a whirlpool of air while this close to the ground. I had heard about downdrafts and wind-shear effects and had dealt with them several times before, but then, I was at least 4,000 feet above the ground, giving me lots of room to react and for the plane to respond. This time, after leveling the plane, the left wing dropped and the plane kept dropping, and the ground was getting closer. I knew I had to try to control the plane!

Out the left window, I could see the ground now. It was so close that I felt I could reach out and touch it. I tried leveling the wings again, bringing the right one down. By this time, I knew that we were going to crash. I told my passengers to brace themselves as I kept trying to control the plane. My heart was pumping out of my chest as I leveled it out. Everything seemed to be happening in slow motion, and I had a sensation of the plane leaning slightly to the left and forward as we crashed. Then everything went dark.

When I regained consciousness, I was hanging upside down and covered in dirt. My head rested against the yoke of the plane. I was dizzy, and my face and head hurt. I could barely push away from the yoke because my left arm was throbbing so. I could see the ground underneath through the broken roof of the plane and realized we had flipped. Later, I would find out that, though we had landed somewhat level, the plane's momentum rolled us forward to a down slope, which flipped us.

I wanted to see what happened to the others, but I couldn't see out of my left eye and I knew I shouldn't move because of the potential for spinal injury. Otherwise, I remembered almost nothing of these moments. If I called out, I couldn't hear a response because my ears were ringing and it was so loud in the cockpit. All I saw was dirt and white foam beneath me. "Was this foam something that deployed in the crash?" I thought. "Where are Steve, Lindsay, and her friend?"

I tried moving by pulling my legs out, but I was trapped. I couldn't feel them, either. All my pain was in my head, neck, and left arm. My next thought was, "Oh my God, how are my family and my daughter's friend?" I yelled out to them, but got no response. "Are they dead?" I wondered, "Most people don't survive plane crashes. Wait, am I alive? What if my husband, daughter, and friend are dead?" I couldn't bear that thought. Fear was inching into me, along with tears.

I called out to my passengers again. I could faintly hear the girls talking to someone, but I couldn't make out the words. I tried opening my eyes, but I must have blacked out again. Time seemed to be standing still. I had no idea how long I had been hanging there trying to understand what was going on. I wasn't sure where I was or what had happened. I just knew that I couldn't move, and I was in immense pain as I tried to brush the dirt out of my eyes. As I looked at my right hand, I saw that it was dirty and bloody. But more important to me was my breathing. "Why am I having such a hard time breathing?" I thought.

My thought process was all over the map. I kept asking myself the questions of "where are we, how did we get here, why can't I move, where are our rescuers?" It seemed like it was taking days to get help. I could barely hear my daughter's voice with another girl, who was laughing and talking loudly. I could also hear a man talking to the girls. Unfortunately, I couldn't see them or make out what they were saying.

Focused efforts of extricating the passengers

I must have blacked out again, because I awoke to a firefighter touching my arm and asking me questions. He was talking to me from outside the plane. It finally sunk in that he was telling me not to move and that they were going to have to cut the plane away in order to get me out. Although he was trying to be nice, he was asking me what I perceived to be dumb questions like "what happened" and "what time is it?" My thinking was: It's obvious what time it is and we were in a plane crash!

He explained that he would crawl in and try to get me out. Another firefighter came over, and the two of them used chainsaws and "the jaws of life" to get to me. The machinery was so loud that my head felt as if it were exploding.

I realized then that I had heard the girls, but I still hadn't heard from Steve. Where was my husband? The next thing I heard was, "Don't move as we support you to lower you down. First, we will undo your seatbelt and lower you onto the backboard. We will continue to do more assessments of you and then strap you to the backboard," a firefighter said. "What? I must not be in good condition," I thought, since I knew exactly what this meant. As a ski patrol instructor, I had been on a backboard many times in training for our students on the mountain. I knew that the use of a backboard meant I could have severe injuries.

While trying to extricate me, someone held my head still, while two people positioned themselves on either side of me and a fourth undid my seatbelt. I could feel them gently lowering me down. I was glad that they were gentle; I was in so much pain. "Was childbirth easier?" I thought, as I still couldn't catch my breath.

They must have turned me as they laid me on the backboard. My back was screaming in pain and my head throbbing. But what was so strange to me was that, despite so much pain, my legs didn't hurt at all. Through the one eye that could see, I tried to look down at my feet, but the firefighter holding my head resisted my movement. He told me that another firefighter was reaching for my right foot since somehow it was upside down. What I couldn't see was that my foot was a mess: Most of the skin at the arch was torn away, with bones and tendons showing. Also, when the second firefighter turned my foot so it was facing right side up, I didn't feel any pain. It was slowly dawning on me that I had what we called in medical response "compromised sensation and motor function" from nerve damage to my back. And my breathing seemed to get more painful and difficult when the straps for the backboard were tightened across my chest. We found out later that one of my seven broken ribs had punctured my lung. No wonder the straps hurt so much and seemed to make my breathing more difficult.

I asked the firefighter by my head what was going on with me, but he just answered that they were taking good care of me. When I explained that I was a ski patrol instructor right there at Northstar, he told me that my right foot was in bad shape. Later, I would learn that I had been pinned in the plane by the rudders from the engine coming into me. The firefighters knew I was paralyzed when I had no reaction to the realignment of my foot.

Soon, more rescuers arrived. Although a few of them knew me from our shared mountain patrolling experiences, they didn't even recognize me at first. It was comforting to me, though, to be in their hands. Before too long, we heard the CareFlight helicopter overhead. I still hadn't seen any of my passengers but was told not to worry—that they were being sent as a precaution to the local hospital. This news lessened my anxiety somewhat.

The flight nurse turned out to be my friend Emily. She explained that they would be flying me to Renown Trauma Center in Reno. It would take about 15 minutes. As we took off, I discovered that I wasn't afraid at all of flying so soon after the crash. Although I was feeling very loopy, I was just disappointed that I couldn't see out from the backboard with an oxygen mask on my face. That's how much I loved flying and still do!

Later, I found out that there were several police on the scene as well as two fire engines. Each rescuer had his or her own responsibilities: While firefighters were working with me, others were taking care of Steve and the girls. They had to wait until they got me out to be able to get to the girls. At least they knew that the girls were in stable shape since their communication was good. The girls had unfastened their seat belts and fallen to the ground a few feet away, since the plane was upside down. But the metal of the crumpled airplane still kept them trapped.

One firefighter found Steve walking around aimlessly looking for help. He was very confused. Under normal circumstances, Steve would have been taking care of us, since he was an EMT (Emergency Medical Technician). The firefighters got him to lie down so they could do a full physical assessment to find any signs of what his injuries might be. When the firefighters asked him questions, though, he had no recollection of the crash or what was going on. He thought that he might have blacked out. There was no sign of physical injury, thankfully. But as a precaution, they put him on a backboard too. Once he was secured, they left a policeman with him to keep him calm and watch to see if his cognitive ability improved.

I learned later that an off-duty policeman who had seen the crash had rushed to the scene and come to Lindsay's window, trying to get her to stay belted upside down until the paramedics could assess her injuries. Lindsay's friend was already on the ground, having released her own seatbelt. The policeman knelt outside the plane, holding Lindsay's hand. If he weren't there, she likely would have been hysterical.

When Lindsay finally couldn't bear being upside down any longer, she released her belt and fell to the ground alongside her friend. The policeman continued to comfort them as the buzz saws worked on the wreckage to extricate us. This angel of a policeman comforted my daughter as she saw me carried away to the helicopter.

By now, the firefighters had created a big enough hole to maneuver towards the girls. There was just enough room for three firefighters to take one girl out at a time. Since Lindsay's friend was closest, they checked her out first. She complained of a headache and pain in her finger, but because she might have a concussion, the firefighters followed protocol and backboarded her. As soon as they moved her out of the plane, the other firefighters went to Lindsay. She was presenting with a deep, bloody cut on her shoulder and a head injury as well as confusion, since she didn't remember what happened. One firefighter held her head to stabilize her spine in case she had a spinal injury. By this time, Lindsay was so scared that she was trembling. She was fourteen and had just seen her mom being taken to a helicopter and wasn't sure where or how her dad was.

The firefighters strapped her onto a backboard, too, and carried her to the fire ambulance, where she met up with her father. On separate backboards, they couldn't even hug each other. Lindsay's friend was on another fire ambulance on her way to the hospital already.

Although Tahoe Forest, the local Truckee hospital, was just down the street, it seemed to take forever to reach it.

We were lucky to be alive, especially since the plane was crumpled and most people don't survive a plane crash. At the airport where we crashed, we were fairly close to an access road near the runway. The brother of a CareFlight nurse was working at the airport office and listening to the airport's radio. Thankfully, he called the crash in immediately in order to get the medical personnel en route. The first rescuers arrived in less than six minutes.

Chapter 2
Recovery in the Hospital

With traumatic injuries, I faced the challenges of recovery as a paraplegic.

On the way to the hospital in the ambulance, Steve called my brother, Curtis Weinman, who was also a pilot. He also called a dear friend, Bruce Barry, who thankfully called a few friends and our sons who lived in different cities in California. My parents were in Europe on vacation and unable to rush home. So, Curtis and his wife Erin drove eight hours overnight from Utah to be with us, not knowing what our conditions were and whether I would live or die.

When I arrived at Renown in the helicopter, another miracle happened. Emily, the flight nurse, brought me in and had to convince the receiving physician assistant, Dan Coll, that it was me. He was a good friend but didn't recognize me because I was covered in dirt, with a swollen, bloody and deformed face. With convincing, he finally realized it was me. He took outstanding care of me, moving promptly and arranging the support I needed. I was so lucky to have a friend at the hospital.

I was in bad shape. The X-rays showed that my spine was broken in a number of places, including one burst vertebra, causing paralysis. I also had bilateral brain injuries, with bleeding in my frontal lobes (cognitive portion). One of my seven broken ribs punctured my lung. And I had broken bones on my face, foot, and legs as well. What a mess!

The hardest part for me was not knowing what was going on with my passengers or even me. Being alone for the first twelve hours in the hospital didn't help. I had no idea of the extent of injuries of my passengers.

Our two sons, TJ and Andrew, rushed to get to Reno and picked up Steve, who had been released from the Truckee hospital, to come with them to see me. Lindsay had been transferred via ground ambulance to the same trauma hospital where I was already. And her friend was held just for observation, in Truckee hospital, a little longer because she was a minor. What a relief it was to see Steve and the boys. By the time my family arrived, I had already had my surgeries and was still really out of it from the injuries and medication. Steve updated me on the other passengers' conditions. What a huge relief for me to know how well they were. I could deal with whatever my condition was; but if I had changed their lives, I wasn't sure how I would be able to deal with it.

For me, I was "smooshed." The medical language for my surgeries went like this: C6 was broken, so the doctors went into the side of my neck to fuse C5, C6, and C7 together. My right foot was open (degloved)

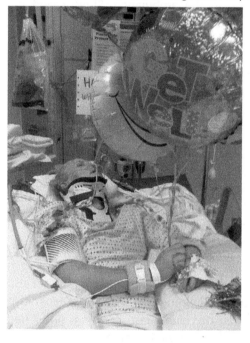 at the arch near the heel, with fractured foot bones and fractured tibia/fibula, so they had to screw the bones together. My thoracic spine at T12 was burst, so they fused T11 to L1, putting in a cage to support my spine. This was the injury that stayed with me, making me a paraplegic. They also put in an IVC filter (clot catcher) in a major vein. Because the other bone breaks were hair-line fractures, they did not require surgery. Luckily, I had a congenital fusion on cervical spine at C1 and C2 (which I am told saved my life).

After evaluation and x-rays at her first hospital, the doctors found that Lindsay had a hairline fracture on her vertebrae in her back and was transferred by ambulance to my hospital, Renown. The doctors there decided to do a spinal fusion. By the time Steve and the boys had arrived at Renown Hospital, Lindsay's surgery was completed, so they were able to comfort her. I didn't see her for a couple more days because of her own recovery. Steve rushed over to see her in the children's ward and was happy to find her smiling and laughing with some of our friends from the ski patrol.

Lindsay was recovering on the children's floor of the hospital and I was in the Critical Care Unit at Renown. A number of friends came in to check on us, which was so thoughtful. Our friends and family had to go back and forth to visit us. When my parents came back into the country from their vacation, they immediately made their way to Reno finding their two girls out of their surgeries. By the time they got there, Lindsay was already healing up and I started becoming more interactive.

This period at Renown was especially uncomfortable. I couldn't tolerate being touched because I was so bruised and broken. It was also difficult because of my neck, chest, and leg braces, plus, I had to deal with the reality of paraplegia. I couldn't feel or move my legs, making it even more difficult to move in bed.

At first, I could barely communicate and had restraints on, because I was trying to pull out the IV and feeding tubes in me. I must have set off the alarms because the nurses came rushing in and tied me down to the bed. Because of my brain injury, I actually believed that I needed to demonstrate how brave and courageous I was.

Then I graduated to talking incessantly about imaginary business deals (my work is in real estate). I had at least two stories or plans a day, with varying themes. One of my favorites was a plan for building a shopping mall in Bangkok. I insisted that Steve write it down and was annoyed when he wouldn't do it right away. I kept yelling at him to go get a pen and paper. Finally, he started writing as I dictated very detailed and explicit ideas of what I wanted. Again, I was adamant that Steve stay focused and capture all of the details. This Bangkok open-air shopping mall had to be perfect with the correct placement of units and the right amount of retail stores and restaurants. I was making layout plans, creating timing for openings, and recommending how the stores should be managed and run. I only wished they had kept the plans; maybe they would have been useful.

After two weeks at Renown, I was transferred to Santa Clara Valley Medical Center (VMC) in San Jose. On a stretcher, I was loaded by the crew onto the air ambulance in order to fly to the local trauma center nearest my home. When our plane took off, I again was so happy that I still loved to fly. I could have just stayed up in the air all day, especially since Steve was with me.

That was the day, a Monday, that I began to feel more alert and yet more pain—the meds were wearing off or at least lessened. Upon arrival at VMC, because of my head injury, I was placed in the head injury unit. Unfortunately, I would doze off trying to recover only to be awoken by others screaming. I couldn't seem to get any sleep there because of the noise level as well as constant activity from sharing a room. Since I had both a head and a spinal injury, the next day I was moved downstairs to the spinal unit.

I lucked out again. My spinal doctor, Dr. James Crew, was relatively new and was on top of his game. All of the hospital staff knew I was an EMT, so they treated me like a professional, which I really appreciated. I wanted to know the medical side of what was really happening to me. Since I was very curious, I asked many questions, trying to speed up the healing process.

Right after the move downstairs, Dr. Crew diagnosed me with a bacterial infection (MRSA) on my foot. The only good thing that came out of this was getting a private room.

Celebrating Andrew's birthday at VMC
with Lindsay, TJ, and Andrew cloaked in hospital gowns

The MRSA on my foot kept my visitors cloaked in hospital gowns and added to the challenge of my healing. I felt that Dr. Crew saved my foot, since he was watching it closely to manage the infection. He knew that I could easily lose it and brought in four different specialists to look at it. One time all four doctors came in at once, and one of these doctors had a cavalier attitude regarding the infection. He had the audacity to say to me that if the foot got any more infected, they would just cut the lower leg off, since I couldn't walk anyway. Can you imagine?

That doctor assumed that I wouldn't be walking. But what he didn't realize was that I need both of my legs whether I walked or not. I use them for standing, walking in parallel bars, horseback riding, and simple transfers that I do all the time. Without my leg, I couldn't have done any of it, or at least it would have been more difficult to adapt.

I need my leg!

In the hospital, there were shift changes during the day. Because of my condition, I needed a lot of help and had to turn to the nurses. I always perked up when a fabulous nurse, Vicki Anderson, came on the floor. She helped me get through the hospital stay and answered many of what probably seemed like stupid questions. She really made a difference for me.

As long as I can remember, I have also needed my sleep. I was always envious of those friends or colleagues that could get away with five or six hours a night; I needed eight hours or I was a grump! Thankfully, the night nurses would let me sleep straight from midnight to 6:00 in the morning. Then, they would get my vitals and a few other things and allow me to go back to sleep. It seemed that I needed twelve hours of sleep for my recovery. And, I really was too sleepy to move until about 10:00 am. I guess it was the healing that required so much sleep, because I had always been a morning person before, but I certainly wasn't in the hospital.

Because of the hemorrhages in my brain, in both frontal lobes, the doctors were worried about my mental acuity recovery. To help me improve and test my recovery, a psychologist worked with me every day playing games. The focus of the games was to challenge my cognitive lobes. The games were simple for me, since they were math word problems and I was good at math. Yet, whereas before the accident, I would have gotten all of these problems correct in a short amount of time, in the hospital I didn't. My learning and behavior were not my normal, so the medical team was really worried about me and watched me closely.

Getting out of bed wasn't fun; I had to have help to get in my wheelchair. In the afternoon as part of my healing, I did physical therapy every day in the rehab gym. I must have looked like an alien with neck, chest, and leg braces enveloping my body. The physical therapist, Liz, would help me with various exercises for upper-body strength, and stretching and rolling for my lower body. As time went on, Liz had me doing more aggressive exercises. I was working hard pushing weights, pulling down overhead bars, and pushing out. Sitting in my wheelchair and leaning forward, I grabbed the bar and with outstretched arms I pulled the weights towards me. I repeated the process with fifteen repetitions and then stopped. Although Liz told me to do ten repetitions, I would do fifteen reps. And, I would do three cycles for each of my exercises. Because of my broken foot, I wasn't allowed to stand, so I just worked out my arms and shoulders. It was such hard work to do the simplest tasks, but I would push through them. I had been quite athletic all of my life, so I knew the drill!

Liz helped motivate all the patients having physical therapy by tricking us to do silly things and then singing to us. This enthusiastic encouragement got us into the mood, as she would give me more difficult and creative exercises including working my core. I was frustrated since I lived in a restrictive neck brace and trunk brace; I couldn't move the way she showed me. We had to improvise some of the exercises in order for me to have a good work out. I must have looked funny moving like an Iguana and bending at my waist and curling around. One of the exercises involved simply sitting and catching a ball and then throwing it back, but it was a struggle. I would almost fall over, many times. Who would have thought that throwing a ball would be so hard?

Together we did a lot of stretching and movement, like rotating my legs and hips. Liz was very positive and encouraging. After two weeks, I was getting stronger when the therapy came to a screeching halt because Dr. Crew found that I had developed HO (*Heterotopic ossification*), an abnormal bone growth, in both hips. In the left hip, the crystallization was so built up that the doctors were worried that it would grow into and lacerate my femoral artery, which would be fatal. This setback was disappointing. The successes in physical therapy with my degree of injury and paralysis were hard won and too easily lost, it seemed.

At the end of the training each day, a small group of us would gather to roll through the first floor of the hospital. One of the physical therapists tried to make it fun, but at the time I didn't see the point of rolling through the halls. Little did I know that it was training to get us ready to be out in the "real world" and get us rolling.

Near the end of my stay at this hospital, Liz would have me do what I thought were the silliest of exercises—wheelies going over little pieces of wood. I couldn't figure out why I had to practice them. Later, when I got home, I learned why: I needed to do wheelies to get over curbs and ruts in floors and sidewalks.

Most of my operations were performed at Renown, but I had two while I was at VMC. The first was when I was taken by ambulance to a critical care dental appointment. I had cracked my two front teeth in the crash, and it was becoming very difficult to eat; so, after four weeks in the hospital, I needed to get the teeth fixed. The second surgery was to remove the IVC filter, a clot catcher in my femoral artery that I had from my spinal surgery. I had a choice of taking it out or being on blood thinners for the rest of my life. I chose to take it out just before I was to leave the hospital, though I was warned that the attempt might not be successful at VMC.

During the surgery to remove the IVC filter, I had another surprise; I woke up! I could hear the surgeons discussing their efforts! I had read about this happening with other patients during surgery, but it was quite a disquieting experience. Worse yet was that in the end their efforts failed, and I needed to have a second surgery (the same one) at Stanford Hospital soon after I got out of Valley Medical Center. Again, I awoke during the second attempt, hearing the nurses talk. I couldn't believe that I had to do the same surgery twice; at least this second operation was successful.

Some of the happier moments during my stay at VMC occurred when the competitive soccer team that I had been coaching came to visit, in their uniforms, to wish me well. We had trained much of the summer to get ready for the regular season games, which started that first weekend after Labor Day. Unfortunately, I not only missed the first game, but also the entire fall season. I was so disappointed. Luckily, we had a great assistant coach, Jon Cohan, who stepped up with my trainer, Bav

Thakrar, to keep the girls strong and play the games. During their visit, it was so wonderful to go out to the courtyard of the hospital so that all the players could sit around me. Seeing their bright enthusiastic faces put tears in my eyes. It was so thoughtful and touching that I am sure it sped up my recovery.

Mountain Lions Soccer Team in courtyard at VMC

Also, the hospital staff had a few people in wheelchairs come to visit me. It was helpful to meet active paraplegics since I had no idea what to expect. We talked about the activities that they could do and discussed what we thought I might be able to do, such as scuba diving. We also took an outing to Starbucks. I was with patients who were much worse off than I was, and it was humbling. The big lesson of the trip was the extra time it took to do everything—loading and unloading from vehicles, for instance.

The hospital staff was committed to teaching us a new way of life. We had to learn to give ourselves more time and use techniques to do the everyday functions we took for granted previously, like transferring from bed to chair, managing ourselves in the bathroom and shower, and manually powering our wheelchair if we had the use of our arms. I was so grateful that I could use my arms, and that I had a strong faith, a wonderful husband, and a family to go home to.

Still, I was very curious about what my future life would look like. Would I be able to get around, keep working (especially with the brain injury), and do any of the physical activities that I had so enjoyed before? I really wasn't sure about how life would work from a wheelchair. A college friend asked her wheelchair-bound friend, Sharon Kelleher, to come and give me a sneak preview of what my new life would be like. She came to visit the week before I was released and told me that she had been in a car crash and been in the same hospital fifteen years earlier.

The encouraging thing was that she could basically do everything that an able-bodied person could do, but she did it adaptively. She was even ranked No. 7 in the nation in adaptive tennis. Sharon was amazing! Plus she traveled, including a honeymoon trip on an African safari. Steve and I were big travelers, and this news thrilled me. She advised me to keep pushing myself through all of the challenges ahead.

"Life is 10 percent what happens to you and 90 percent how you react to it."

~ Charles R. Swindoll

When I was wheeled out of the hospital a few days afterward, the view of the mountains gave me a new sense of freedom. The neck and foot braces were gone, and I only had to deal with my torso brace. I was making progress, inch by inch.

I would slowly learn what a long road of "recovery" was ahead. It would tax my psychological and physical strength in order to reach my goal of full-out adaptive living.

Chapter 3
The Long Road of Rehab

Focused on healing, I tried many modalities.

Driving into the driveway at our home after being gone so long (two months) seemed surreal. I really had no idea how my life would evolve or even how I would manage day to day. Although it was wonderful to be out on this beautiful November day with family surrounding me, I thought, "Will I be able to do *anything* as before? Can I still be active?"

As Steve lifted me out of the car and put me into a loaner wheelchair, suddenly I was very concerned about the two steps up to the front door and being able to get into the house. Steve calmed me down, explaining that Brian, a parent from the girls' soccer team that I coached, plus two neighbors, John and Ed, had installed several ramps. Steve pushed me up the beautiful new ramp that looked like a deck. Then once inside, Steve pushed me onto another ramp that connected the family room to the rest of the house. Ah, I could maneuver around my home—I was excited. The only room that I couldn't get into because of the narrow doorframe was the laundry room. No big loss!

I knew that our beautiful master bathroom would not work for me the way it was set up; subsequently I was worried about how we would deal with my personal hygiene. Steve rolled me to the old master bedroom that my middle son Andrew had been living in. To my wonderful surprise, Andrew and TJ were waiting there, because they wanted to show me the renovated adjoining bathroom. The boys had replaced the shower and all the fixtures to create a bathroom that I could use. It was so perfect that I could wheel my chair next to the toilet to transfer and use a shower chair to wheel right into the shower. I was so touched that while I was in the hospital they got the house ready for me. The bathroom was nicely done with cream tiles and all the finishes stretching up to the existing window.

Looking out of that window made me realize how much I missed being outdoors. At VMC, I was able to go out into a courtyard, but it wasn't the same as being out in nature. Before I went back into the bedroom, I had to take a stroll (or rather, a roll) outside. I had forgotten how peaceful it was. Soaking in the sun surrounded by bright green trees and a few colorful rose bushes put a smile on my face. *I was home.* While I was sitting outside enjoying the natural view, our beautiful gray barn cat walked right up to me, looking for a pat. I leaned over my wheels and started stroking Jackie's back. She was purring like crazy, and I felt such a welcome. She didn't care that I was in a wheelchair! On the other hand, my dog wouldn't come near me. Steve had to drag her towards me so that I could say hello.

Settling in was slow for me as I got used to my new normal. Getting around the house and just doing simple tasks took a lot of work. The kitchen wasn't set up for me, so, other than putting a microwave on the counter and setting up a lower cabinet with dishes and some food items, I really couldn't use it much. Even the pantry door was too narrow for my chair to fit through. Luckily, Steve was so sweet and would become our master chef.

I was happy that our bedroom would work out so well. Because of the constant pain that I was in, I tried to lie down as often as I could. For some reason, being out of my chair and lying sideways usually lowered the pain a lot. It seemed that breaking up the sitting every several hours made my pain level tolerable. Plus, resting in my bedroom helped with the wonderful views of trees and mountains. It was serene and peaceful.

I was distressed that my own, new wheelchair wouldn't arrive for three months. I should have received it when I left the hospital. People don't generally understand that "wheelchairs are your legs," so I was very frustrated that I had to wait. When you are a paraplegic, the type of chair matters for your pain levels and mobility. The fit for the chair is similar to a fit for shoes. Imagine having to wear the wrong size shoes for three months!

Although the hemorrhages in my brain had cleared as I left the hospital, the doctor made me promise to see a neuropsychologist and keep working on improvement. Mentally, I still wasn't quite back to myself. Especially at night, I found that I wasn't on my game with the quick wit or response. At home, I tried working on my Spanish (which I was told would be extremely frustrating) and helped Lindsay with her math homework. I was struggling, but I kept at it. I wasn't going to let the injury slow me down!

It was hard to imagine that with paraplegia I could do anything fun, like I used to. I needed to do activities to enjoy and relax. I just couldn't sit still. (It is ironic that I am now sitting all the time in a chair.) I thought, "While my body was healing from the accident, what could I possibly do without my working legs? All the sports that I did used my legs and usually my whole body." I was starting to get sad. "How tough would my life be?" teary eyed I continued to think.

Luckily, Dave Heckley, a friend from real estate and now living in Oregon, gave me lots of advice. He was a paraplegic with my same injury level, dealing with the life changes five years longer than me. He had the same can-do positive attitude and encouraged me to get out and do things. There were many activities that we could do, and for Dave, swimming was his biggest one. I was so lucky to have someone that could give me hope, encouragement, and knowledge about what my body could do.

My focus had to be physical therapy to get my body strong in hopes of doing sports. Soon after my release, the hospital sent Pam, an occupational therapist (OT), and Ron, a physical therapist (PT), to teach me how to get around and keep my body healthy and in shape. I still couldn't stand because I couldn't be weight bearing yet; accordingly, they worked my upper body. Ron also worked on my transfers without using a slide board. We would sit on my bed, and he would show me how to "jump" over to the chair. It was difficult at first, but I finally got it. Ron would also stretch me out, which actually felt good. After the stretching, he had me do sidekicks, bridges, and balance drills. I was weak, but I worked it! I loved exercising.

Shortly after I was out of the hospital, I wanted to continue to exercise more than just once a week. I still had my back brace on; and Dr. Brian Warne, a foot and ankle specialist and good friend, recommended More Clinic in San Jose. There, I found Kristen, who had previously specialized in spinal rehab. Her biggest focus was balance and core, so she started me with upper body exercises. Even ten weeks after the crash, I wasn't yet cleared to stand so that I could do weight-bearing exercises. Kristen noticed my frustration and remarked, "If you never sat still when you were able-bodied, why would you want to sit still now?" She hit it: I never did sit still, so she taught me how to continually move in my chair. That movement not only made me feel better, but it also helped my pain level. It seemed my body just didn't want to be sitting all the time.

She worked my core muscles with sit-ups, bridges, and twists. For my arms, I did bicep curls, triceps' dips, and arm lifts. It was frustrating to be confined to anaerobic exercises. I really wanted to get out and work up a sweat. I wasn't sure that I would ever get to work out hard again! Before the crash, the only real exercise that got my blood pumping was triathlons, especially the running segment. I needed to find my "running" fix now.

Finally, at about twelve weeks out, Dr. Warne checked and then cleared me for weight-bearing exercises. While I was in his office, he also noticed that the big toe on my right (bad) foot was red. It turned out that I had an ingrown toenail. As he took care of the nail, he recommended that I get pedicures regularly to avoid the problem. A silver lining—a prescription for pedicures!

Back at home, Ron showed me how to stand in my new standing frame, explaining that I should stand a minimum of an hour each day, but not more than an hour at any one time. Ron also reminded me how to do wheelies and travel over small logs or wood on the road. The hardest thing I had to learn was how to get back into my wheelchair when I fell out. I asked him, "Why would I ever fall out of my chair?" He said, "Your balance is weighted to the back, so it will be easy to fall backwards going up ramps. If the little front wheels dig in, the chair could flip you forward, too. Lastly, you are still learning all the tricks of wheelchair use, and it might be easier for you to fall out."

Ron showed me two ways to get back in the chair. The only one that worked for me was crawling in face-first. I didn't care how hard it was, or how silly I looked. I just wanted to make sure that I could get back in if I fell out. To learn, I practiced several times, though I hoped that I would never have to use the technique again, because it was so laborious and painful.

The next time I went to physical therapy, Kristen taught me how to stand using a walker. She worked with me to use my quadriceps to push off and stand. I was lucky in that I had some musculature below my injury.

I thought it strange that most of my California physical therapists didn't want to work my legs. It made me feel awful, because I knew that weight-bearing exercises help prevent toxicity build-up and osteoporosis. I understood that the medical industry still didn't really know that much about the brain or spine, so I thought it was logical to focus on prevention along with recovery. I remembered when I got my degree in nutrition that most doctors at that time paid little attention to their patients' nutrition. Now, of course, they understand its importance, especially when people are at both ends of life: infancy and old age.

Kristen was great and "got me." She taught me many exercises that I could do at home, such as:

- Stretches
- Sit-ups
- Bridges
- Push-ups
- Catching and throwing a ball while seated
- Turning side to side from a sitting position
- Bicep curls (using TheraBands at home)
- Bent arm rotating in and out with weights
- Arms extended straight out raising and lowering light weights
- Shoulder shrugging

We got to the point, when I could bear weight and was stronger in my core, where she recommended that I go to a facility that had leg equipment that I could use.

Since I still was working with the wonderful OT, Pam, she was willing to work with me to build up my legs in a therapy pool. It was indoors and had a temperature of about 85 degrees. She put weights on my ankles as I stood, stretched, and kicked sideways and backwards. I was surprised at how much I could do with no gravity opposing my movement. She also set me up to swim adaptively. I tried to use good swim technique with strong strokes, but it wasn't quite the same with a lifesaving belt at my waist. Breathing during freestyle stroking was difficult, since my neck was fused, and it didn't do well being hyperextended or turning. I was also surprised that I didn't have the lung capacity I used to. The punctured lung had taken its toll on my breathing. I did my best, though. It was so wonderful to be in the water doing something—not just "sitting." After the swim, my reward was a hot tub. After Pam and Ron were disallowed to accompany me to the pool rehab center, which had its own therapists, Steve took me, and I started swimming more often.

What would I have done without Steve?

Besides all of my physical therapy, I had to learn to drive with hand controls and how to get in and out of the car. To make sure that I could drive safely this new way, I took a driving class. The instructor, Tim, came to our house with a car already equipped with hand controls. He showed me how to use the controls as we practiced in a close-by parking lot. I felt sixteen years old again. Thank God we were in a parking lot so I didn't hit anything. By my third lesson, I finally got the hang of using my hands to accelerate and brake rather than my feet and received my certificate. About the same time, I found a used car to buy (my car before was a manual transmission with a clutch) and had hand controls installed.

While driving would give me a new freedom, getting into and out of a car was not a graceful sight. In the beginning, I had to slide in and out of a vehicle that was the right height (lower to the ground than many) with a slide board. This is a long, flat board placed between the chair and the car seat for paraplegics to slide over. It was a happy day when I could finally make the transfer without a board (after I bought a replacement car)!

About six months after the crash, I got in to see the outpatient rehab spinal doctor at VMC. I met this doctor, who advised biofeedback and acupuncture in addition to physical therapy. Like many of the doctors I met in the hospital, she tried to prepare me for never walking again. But I resisted, thinking, "You aren't God, so you really don't know my fate." I wished I had asked her at the time, what in my x-rays and MRIs proved that I would never walk. Most doctors I have known go by the textbook. I wished they would offer even a glimmer of hope and not be so predictive. It would encourage their patients more, especially since we know there are people who do walk again, even when their doctors predict they never will. Attitude is everything in my book, and I believe it plays a huge role in health!

When I was accepted to start outpatient therapy, my first physical therapist at VMC worked with me doing several exercises. One of the drills used a white board and skateboard for me to sidekick in and out (with a little help, of course). I was thrilled, because I was finally working specifically on my legs and even better was able to move them a little myself.

My second physical therapist, Stephanie, started with me after only two visits to VMC. She worked my core but also gave me exercises for my legs, including:

- Using their standing frame and doing squats
- Transferring from one mat to a higher mat
- Crawling across all the mats
- Rolling over and over
- Kicking up from a prone and supine position (bent leg and straight leg)
- Bending toes back
- Bicycling on an FES Cycle

Since I was going to training weekly, Stephanie thought that I could really benefit from leg braces. She thought I would like being able to stand up and walk around with them, and I did. But there was a lot of discomfort with them, because they went all the way up my legs to my butt. Although they articulated at the knee, we kept them locked until very late in my use of them. The exercise was to first walk through parallel bars and then, soon after, walk around the unit using a walker. I likened this mobility to moon walking, since I moved across the floor straight-legged. I got so good with the braces that I could walk up and down stairs and stand without holding on. I even went out to dinner using them and made my mom cry when I walked into her birthday party.

The frustrating part about the braces was that the activity didn't help build up or even work my leg muscles. Stephanie measured my leg function when I started with the braces; and then two months later, she found that there wasn't any change. I don't know why I assumed they were working my legs, but of course they weren't. Immediately, I went back to my leg exercises, which did produce some improvement, extremely slowly. Ironically, while this was happening, a patient in the rehab department was feeling down about his own school bicycle accident making him a spinal-cord patient. I was asked to encourage him because he was disheartened by the slow rate of improvement he was experiencing. I stressed the importance of staying positive while training hard and realizing that changes can come. He asked, "How do you not give up?" I replied, "The workouts keep me healthy, and I believe that every part of the improvement matters, even if it is just attitudinal." We went on discussing the training, since he already had partial use of one leg. Then he told me about a place where he did acupuncture and rehab training. Strangely enough, it was the name of a doctor that I had planned to call.

Dr. Zhu is a world-renowned acupuncturist and instructor, specializing in head and spinal-cord injuries using scalp acupuncture followed by therapy. My first visit to see him was so amazing that I made training with him part of my recovery. When I would see him once each week, he would perfectly place the needles in my scalp and body. I could tell that he was at the right points from how it felt and my own knowledge from past study of acupressure and massage (a component of my martial arts training) that use the same points. After removing the needles from my body, but not my scalp, he and another doctor would work with me on exercises for my leg muscles—building the ones I had and assisting those that were weak. As I learned, Dr. Zhu had developed this acupuncture to manually reset the brain. These scalp needles were strategically placed, and then left in up to seventy-two hours, since more time could maximize the benefits, whether it was pain management or helping muscles to fire.

The philosophy of stimulating the brain and then working matching body parts did seem to help me. Using these triggers and then following up with physical therapy was great for stress release, and more importantly I gained slow improvement. My favorite exercise was sitting up and pushing my legs against weights. I believed I was pushing about 50 pounds with my left leg and 25 pounds with my right. I was surprised to have double the strength on my left side, especially since I was right-dominant. With time (years) the more damaged right side matched the strength of the left side. I was improving with the training and was ecstatic. However, the slow improvement did test my patience since it was extremely slow. Dr. James Lu took over for Dr. Zhu, and my favorite exercise became walking in parallel bars. Dr. Lu helped me walk, even if it was just protecting my knees from buckling. He knew how to push me to keep me motivated and continue to train my legs.

I tried to work out at least three times each week. I had learned a long time before in athletic training that it required three workouts a week to maintain a level of fitness, and four times to see improvement. So my focus was laser-sharp on exercise. I went to physical therapy twice a week (VMC and Dr. Zhu), swam in the pool once a week, and worked out at home once a week, besides my standing at home (in a standing frame) every day.

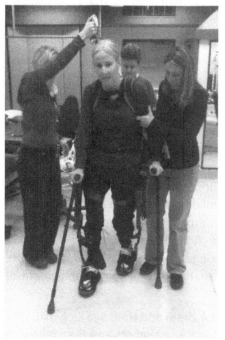

During my VMC physical therapy, I also had an amazing opportunity: I got to walk! VMC was testing a state-of-the-art piece of equipment called eLEGS, designed by Berkeley Bionics. I was VMC'S first test pilot on the equipment. It was a hardware and software system that mechanically walks a paraplegic in an exoskeleton, allowing the brain to translate intent into exoskeleton action. It was so cool that I wished I could take eLegs home.

Although my hospital rehab period came to a close, I had been coaching soccer, learning adaptive sports, volunteering on several boards, and working at APR in real estate... and smiling often said, "I CAN STILL DO IT!" I knew that I had to keep up exercising and wanted to resume more of the physical activity I had so enjoyed in the past. I wasn't sure how much of that activity I could do, but I was going to give it my best effort. This was my goal, and I was determined to fight for it.

Chapter 4
Starting a New Life

*Stepping back into the life I had before the crash
was arduous, yet worth fighting for.*

For a very active person who had become paralyzed, it was hard to imagine doing the same activities I had done before. My idea of fun before the accident was doing different things non-stop. When I was told to relax, I would laugh and explain that activity was what relaxed me. If I were to just sit on a beautiful beach for a long time, for instance, I would go stir crazy. Instead, if I could swim or surf off that beautiful beach, then that was my idea of relaxing. So early on I tried to think of activities I could do without my legs. I began to look into specialty sports and adaptive programs. Although these new sports where different, at least it would give me an opportunity to get out there. Excitedly, I told Steve one morning, "I can do most of the same sports that I did before. I will just have to do them adaptively and relearn them. I can still do them!" (It turns out that the only one I can't do is scuba diving, because of my punctured lung.) He knew that I would be up to the challenge, because he knows I hate the word "can't."

"Attitude is 100 percent of everything you do."
~ Keith Harrell

When I returned to mainstream life, I hit the ground rolling. A month after the release from the hospital I was back up at Lake Tahoe helping our Ski Patrol. And I also went back to my other volunteer activities. To get back into the more physical activities, I had to continue healing and doing my rehab. I really wanted to once again snow and water ski, do other water sports, and ride horses—some of the activities that I had enjoyed at a high level of proficiency much of my life. After the crash, for me to do most of the activities I wanted to do, my equipment and accessories were more complicated and much more expensive, unfortunately. My joke to keep myself motivated was "I must be bored with life; now I get to learn all of these new sports." To be safe, I also needed a buddy during many sports, particularly for horseback riding. Thank goodness I usually had my best friend—my husband. Steve was always beside me to support me physically and emotionally. More than any other, he was the one who made my ambitious program of getting back into my life possible.

I was fortunate, too, to have an extensive network of friends to draw upon for advice and resources as we began our new journey. Luckily and kindly, the four biggest volunteer activities I was doing before the crash remained in place for me.

Our ski patrol directors at Northstar California, Vince Arthur and Mike Fanelli, invited me to come back. Forrest Philpot with the leadership encouraged and chose me to manage the training of new candidates. I could do that position from my chair. Overseeing twenty candidate ski patrollers' training reminded me how much I loved teaching and helping others.

I could not have managed those roles if it weren't for Steve. He helped me get dressed in layers of warm ski clothing to get out the door before daylight each morning. He put batteries in my boots warmers to keep my feet warm. Even with all of this protection and warmth, some days I would come home and my "bad leg"—the one with the broken and plated foot—would be ice cold. To heat me up, Steve would draw a hot bath for me.

Once we got to the mountain, the next challenge appeared. I thought, "How would I get in the gondola when my wheelchair wouldn't fit straight in?" Steve would lift me into the gondola, take the wheels off my chair, hand each one of them to me, and then climb in the gondola with the frame. At the top, he reversed the process. He was so efficient that the gondola operators would just watch and marvel. Steve had created little skis for the front wheels of my chair as well. We often got cheered along as he pushed me through the powder to the ski yurt where I did my trainings.

Most of my body was healing well, although slowly. As my ribs and punctured lung healed, I could breathe more easily, but I couldn't hold as large a volume of air as before. I was also determined not to give up on walking. Though I had been told many times that I would never walk again, I decided to keep working my legs to preserve muscle tone. As my rehab became more frequent, I got stronger at moving my legs out to the sides and pushing against weights.

Even in my early days of recovery, the local Disaster Aid Response Team (DART) had me keep my previous position as the tech rescue team leader, in charge of low and high angle rescue, using rope and pulleys. This was yet another position that pushed me into doing things that I thought someone in a wheelchair wouldn't be able to do—like the day I was teaching rope rescue, and the group didn't remember how to tie a Swiss seat (a harness to attach yourself to a rope for rappelling). I actually took webbing and tied the harness while sitting in my chair. I even surprised myself that I could do it.

Emcee at GOTRSV Fun Run

Another opportunity to give back arose. Being asked to be the treasurer for the Girls on the Run of Silicon Valley (GOTRSV) was wonderful and an honor for me. What was extra special was being the emcee of the 5K fun run, the culmination of the program for girls and young women. I really didn't know how I could continue to be the emcee since I was stationed on a plywood stage. "How could I climb up the ladder to this tall stage," I thought. The organizers of the race built a ramp for me to roll up to the stage: this kindness brought tears to my eyes.

> ## "If we did all the things we were capable of doing, we would literally astound ourselves."
>
> ~ Thomas Edison

Coaching competitive soccer team, Mountain Lions

My assistant coach, Jon Cohan, and trainer, Bav Thakrar, on the girls' competitive soccer team welcomed me back as well. As we started a new season, they provided an affirmation that, though my legs were disabled, I was not! The girls were so amazing to me, too. Before the crash, they would come to me on the field with every little fall or scratch. But now they only came to me when it was important. When I asked why, they said, "Coach, even though you have big injuries, you are still out here. Why would we come and ask about some little bruise or scrape that we can just ignore?" They knew that I was an EMT, so I trusted that they would let me know if something seemed more serious.

Indeed, these activities were as important to me as my work in real estate—selling real estate and managing large offices as a senior vice president. Later, another friend and ex-competitor in the real estate profession, Jeff Barnett, enticed me to come to his company. I had already tried to retire from this profession twice, but it seemed to be in my DNA. The best part of this new position for me was only working part time. I was there to help clients with their real estate needs and build up the agent team—something I had done many times earlier in my career.

Real Estate focus on clients

Between my work and my volunteer activities, I was now pretty busy. I also wanted to continue my physical therapy, focusing on spinal cord injury rehabilitation. Very few places in the country had the expertise, so when my friend Jana suggested Project Walk in Carlsbad, California, I jumped at the opportunity. There, I could do a number of new exercises that they taught me. I was thrilled that I could ride a stationary bike as long as there was no friction against the wheels. Who would have thought? I learned many new exercises, such as:

- Dog and Cat and crawling on all fours by advancing my legs
- Modified push-up, bending at my waist
- Lying down and sitting, twisting my body
- Bouncing on a Bosu ball
- "Walking" on a treadmill, in a gait machine
- "Standing upright" in a vibration machine; even my nose tickled
- Riding a stationary bike

After training at Project Walk, we started to assemble some equipment at home that would help in my rehab. My favorite was the parallel bars that my son TJ welded for me to "walk" in. As recommended by my first PT at VMC, Steve also set up a skateboard and a white board that would allow me to do side-kicks. (I would roll the skateboard with my legs over a whiteboard placed on top of the bed to do these.) The most interesting piece of equipment for me to use was a vibrating platform beneath my feet. The vibration always felt good on my legs! Eventually, we even purchased a refurbished FES cycle, though our insurance declined to pay for it. Pedaling on this bike was one of the best exercises for working my legs. I would bicycle with electrodes attached to my legs, firing electrical stimulation into my muscles which contracted them to help me peddle faster. Sometimes, I actually worked up a sweat. I have now logged over 5,000 "miles" on this cycle.

For months, my friend, Niki, had encouraged me to do some rehab on horseback. She had been volunteering at One Step Closer (OSC), a stable where they do such training for people with many types of injuries and medical conditions. Niki had given me a pair of old riding pants. My helmet was less elegant—my search-and-rescue helmet. The facility was next to a historic home and a lake where I used to water ski.

When we arrived, the owner/trainer, Landa, came over to introduce herself and tell me what to expect. Would you believe that there was a ramp to wheel up to the side of a horse for people in a wheelchair? Of course, it wasn't just any horse, mind you, but a patient one that could deal with poor or incorrect physical commands. This horse, named Reba,

was saddled with a special bareback saddle. I needed help to get on, even with the ramp. Once on Reba, I had a lead person to guide the horse plus two side walkers with me in case I lost my balance. But soon, I was sitting tall, feeling like the Queen of the World on this horse. All the joy of my years of riding came back to me as our procession started into the arena.

Once a week, I went to this stable, getting stronger and better every time. I started to learn dressage, becoming more consistent and smooth with every lesson. As I improved, the trainer added more challenges.

One day, Reba and I were to walk up and over a platform. As we approached it, she took the first step up, and I started to fall off. Niki, who was side-walking with me, pushed me back up before I fell to the ground. On a much later ride, my friend was encouraging me by pointing to the hills "where one day soon," she promised, "we will ride on the trails if I work hard."

Key Note Speaker at OSC

I wouldn't have thought that as a paraplegic I would get as many firsts as when I was an able-bodied person. But I did have one at this equine therapy facility. They asked me to be a keynote speaker on what I had accomplished at their annual program—on horseback! While I had gotten used to riding English style, holding the reins in both hands, I figured I should present Western style (one-handed), since I talk a lot with my hands. Luckily, when the day came, Reba stood very still. It was thrilling to ride into the center of the arena to make my presentation.

The most wonderful surprise was learning to ride the quarter horse that my friend Sue had given me just before the accident. Now I had my own horse to ride whenever I wanted. Although the horse, Josie, had been trained as a hunter jumper, in dressage, and in trail riding, she had to learn how to work with me, especially since my commands were different than she was used to, and I couldn't use my legs or heels. We took Josie down to OSC for several weeks for her to be vetted as "bombproof" for me to ride. Once Josie was ready for me, we worked her in the arena at OSC, doing mostly dressage-style patterns. It was so much fun to be able to go from post to post, over platforms, and more. In fact, I was doing so well (probably helped a little by riding before the crash) that the trainer, Landa, told me I could compete with able-bodied riders in the basic dressage level. Although that sounded intriguing and I was a competitive sort, I loved trail riding best.

By this point, I had become strong and stable enough to ride the trails. I started off slow with someone, usually Steve, leading the horse. With time and training in the countryside riding at many of the beautiful local parks, I became a better rider. I built my skills up, thanks to friends, especially Niki and Kathleen, who were some of my teachers. Eventually, thanks to Kathleen, we acquired another horse, a Tennessee Walker, Gem, to the mix. Having two horses was great, since Steve could ride his own and not have to "borrow" a horse.

After a while, we rode on long trails, not only gaiting and cantering, but also galloping up hills. In my wildest dreams, I didn't think that I would be able to ride that hard. Eventually, I was in good enough condition to take a ride for six hours. Since that length of ride was a first for me even as an able-bodied rider, I was thrilled. I wasn't new to riding, and it was so rewarding and refreshing to be able to accomplish real-life riding like I did in high school. Surprisingly, *I CAN STILL DO IT!*

I think back to when I was a girl of fourteen, my family moved to Los Gatos. Our new home had a horse stable, since the previous owners liked to ride. After asking for a horse and being turned down, I was so happy when my father decided to board horses and allowed me to manage the stable. Wow! He and I spent a lot of time together fixing fences,

straightening the barn, and readying the pastures. When the horses came, I put them in stalls and paddocks based on how they interacted with each other. Before school every morning, I would feed the horses their hay and fill their individual water buckets. The horses were so focused on their meal that they pranced excitedly when they saw me coming. What a nice welcome to the day! Of course, the other part of the work was not so much fun: cleaning the stalls.

Getting ready to ride the local trail

One of the boarders had a champion quarter horse and allowed me to ride her. I used to ride her bareback with just a halter—no reins, bit, or saddle. One Saturday morning during the summer a year after our move, I prepared her to go for a ride. I put a halter on her, checked her hooves, and began to groom her. I combed her shiny black mane to get out any knots, and then switched to a brush to smooth out her chest, back, legs, and neck. After she was primped, she was ready to go. I jumped on her bareback and headed out of the barn.

To warm her up for our ride, we walked around the outside perimeter of the fence in our lower field. When she started to canter, my dog Shep took off towards us from the house, spooking the horse so much that she went into a full gallop, heading towards the creek. Shep chased after us, nipping at the horse's tail. I hung onto her mane and pinched my legs hard against her sides. I could barely hang on! As we raced toward the creek, two choices became apparent: go straight through the trees into the creek or make a sudden 90-degree turn. The horse (Ginger) made the choice before I could, and we veered hard right. Or I should say, she did as I went straight ahead, landing on my butt in rocks, grass, and oak leaves. Aside from some minor cuts, scrapes, and bruises on my arms, I was okay, though. I got up and ran after the horse so I could calm her down. Shep ran back up to the house, sensing she had done something wrong.

My daughter, Lindsay, once told me I am like a cat with nine lives. I have used five so far: falling out of a tree house, surviving ovarian and thyroid cancers, the plane crash, and spinal meningitis. Not to mention I had to deal with a few other injuries like ACL replacement, toe and hand surgery, and a severely sprained ankle.

Taking educated risks has always been about living life with full engagement for me. Physical exercise is almost as important to me as breathing. During this time of starting my new life, I learned to appreciate the simpler pleasures of life too: just being outdoors, doing productive work, and being with family and friends.

I am thrilled at how much I have been able to reclaim the activities of my able-bodied life. The new word in my vocabulary is adaptive. *It really isn't new, because I had to adapt all the time earlier in my life, whether it was in real estate or rescue. With the right equipment and accessories, I have been able to continue engaging in the physical exercise and sports that I love.*

Chapter 5
Meeting the Challenge
of Change

Dealing with tough situations, our family had a
penchant for positivism which helped us through the
struggles to adapt to our "new normal."

My family

For me to heal after the crash, I wanted to be surrounded with the positives—I didn't have room for negative energy. Fortunately, the support I got from my family was huge, even though we all knew that our life together would be different, and we would have to adapt. My husband, our children, and my parents all dealt with each situation as it arose, trying to find the best result. I am so grateful that my parents had raised me to be positive—to find the best in life. I hadn't realized that I had done the same with my kids. And I didn't fully appreciate this quality in my family until long after the crash. I can only imagine how hard it was for my parents to see their only daughter "smooshed" by the downed plane. Insult was added to injury when the crash happened on my dad's birthday.

Thank God everyone in the plane survived, and my parents got to see how active I became after the crash. At first, it shook up my mother a little. The biggest evidence of her feelings came after I was at the second hospital, where Steve had posted family photos in my room. One included a photo of our Cessna with my daughter, and my mom wondered if I minded seeing it  there. She was concerned that it might disturb me. But I didn't mind seeing it at all. I loved flying, and it reminded me of how much fun we had taking family trips, even across country in our private plane.

Luckily, in this second hospital, my mom stepped in to be my advocate, asking the doctors lots of questions, ensuring that I would get the best care. We found out how important it is to have an advocate.

My brother, Curtis, also a pilot, drove straight to the hospital from Utah when he got the news of the crash. He was the first one at my hospital bed, since Steve and our sons hadn't reached me there yet. Curtis was quite distraught when he saw my condition and heard the prognosis: "She will never walk again." He knew how active I had been and how much my life would change. It was so comforting for me that he was there to support me during the first week. Curtis was so good with Lindsay, too. Because Lindsay was injured in the crash, her doctors chose to give her a spinal fusion.

Lindsay had the hardest time, probably because she was the youngest—a freshman in high school. When she was strong enough to walk with a walker soon after her own surgery, she came to visit me, usually with another family member. After I was moved to VMC, it must have been hard for her to see her mother so incapacitated; she didn't come very often while I was hospitalized. Later on, she confided to me that she was at a loss about what to say or how to act. She knew my injuries were serious and wasn't sure how I would recover. Her biggest fear was the unknown. Our sons came to visit me when they could, since TJ was at college three hours south of us, and Andrew was working two jobs, though still living at home.

Lindsay didn't complain about my being unable to do the things I could before the crash. She appreciated my continued coaching of her competitive soccer team and attendance at her cheerleading events. And she was always positive and helpful getting me into and out of the car. But when it came to personal things, like braiding my hair, she was the typical teenager—too busy to help. And, when she saw that I could do it myself, she was relieved.

The crash left her terrified of flying at first, and she refused to take her first flight with Steve or me. That crushed me. We knew that she would probably never fly in a small plane again but would have to figure out a way to get on a commercial plane. About seven months after the crash, her high-school fashion class had a field trip to Los Angeles. It would be only an hour-long flight, but Lindsay still wasn't sure that she could do it. Her teacher was kind enough to make an exception for her, allowing her best friend Danielle to go on the trip with the class. While Lindsay was fine boarding the plane, when she heard the engines cranking up, she started crying. She was thrilled that she had her best friend and a classmate on either side of her, squeezing her hands. Once in the air, she relaxed a bit; however, on the return flight, she had the same reactions. It would take a while before she was less fearful.

One of Lindsay's frustrations was a feeling that she lost the opportunities her brothers had to do more adventurous travel. After the accident, we still travelled by RV or on a cruise ship, but she missed some of the adventures and excursions that we used to take, especially compared to the trips her brothers went on with Steve and me, like bicycling, climbing, hiking, scuba diving, and windsurfing.

When TJ was told about the crash and that I might not survive, he drove up from college. Luckily, before he picked up his brother and reached the hospital, he learned that I was in stable condition. But when he and his brother first saw me with my doctor and other family members, he fainted. TJ stayed at the hospital until I was through the surgeries and stable again. Then, he had to get back to college and take Andrew back to work.

The excitement of Christmas morning

Of all three of our children, TJ was the one who believed in making life as easy as possible, so he complained that I wouldn't buy a mini-van with a ramp so that I could just roll in and out of it. He thought it was ridiculous that I wouldn't give myself that convenience rather than breaking down my wheelchair and reassembling it or calling for help each time I went to the office or other location. Since I refused to drive a van and it was actually faster to break down my chair than use a lift, I had no interest in that option. Besides, my car had the power to drive in the hills!

Andrew was working so much that we rarely saw him, but he tried to be around for me when Steve wasn't home. In the beginning, it always seemed that I had my medical issues or would fall out of my chair when Steve was gone. And, at these times, Andrew was so helpful and comforting, working with me to clean up and take care of the issues. If I were crying, he would comfort me, telling me how much he appreciated me. His comments would help me forget about the challenges.

Several times when I fell out of my wheelchair no one was home, and I would call on Andrew or my parents to help. Not wanting to be dependent, twice when it happened, I eventually solved the issue before they had to come running. Luckily, I remembered what my PT had taught me about how to get back in my wheelchair. I had to take the cushion off first and put it over my footplate to protect me. Then I had to push up onto my knees, like kneeling, which was the hardest to do, lining up my legs and stabilizing them. Finally, I would drag myself up into the chair and flip around. On the rare occasion that I did fall out when no one was around, it took me about twenty minutes to get back in. It was so much easier when Steve was around and could just lift me back into the chair, especially since it seemed that I fell out so often.

Steve's first reaction to our crash was "Thank God we are all alive." When he finally received the information that Lindsay was okay and I was out of surgery, he could take a breath. Then, when it became apparent that no one knew and most doubted whether I would ever walk again, Steve decided to just deal with each situation as it came along. During Lindsay's and my hospital stay in Reno, it was tough on him because he had to jump between both of our rooms to keep abreast of our recovery. Since he was not home in his own bed, but staying at a local hotel or at the hospital, he wasn't getting enough sleep. He was exhausted. It was enough to deal with one day at a time rather than pondering the future.

Once back at home, besides juggling without me, he had to get the house ready for a wheelchair and all of the other adjustments my paraplegia would necessitate. Although some things got missed—like paying a few bills on time—Steve kept his eye on the essentials, like getting Lindsay back in school and settled. And he visited me every day when I was at VMC. Once I was home, he did a lot of the household work that I used to do, like cooking, doing the laundry, and juggling the finances.

My husband Steve is a gem.

Even the simplest tasks could turn out poorly, if we didn't keep our senses of humor. Cooking was especially dicey, which we learned on the day when Lindsay and I decided to surprise Steve with his favorite dish of Eggs Benedict when he came home from teaching. Lindsay had purchased the ingredients, and I set about to make the Hollandaise sauce and cook the Canadian bacon. She was assigned to toast the English muffins and poach the eggs. But she wasn't comfortable with the poaching operation. I tried it. What a failure: First, I could barely reach over the saucepan to get the eggs placed in the boiling water. Then, we overcooked them because I couldn't get them out of the pan, so Lindsay had to do it.

One of the things that I wondered about in the hospital was what my physical relationship with my husband would be now that I was a paraplegic. I was reassured when I realized that intimacy is mostly psychological. My husband and I were still in love with each other when the accident happened, and we have carried that love forward.

As soon as I recovered enough to do sports and athletics, Steve worked side by side with me—whatever it took. Having been an Army Special Forces officer, he had the strength to lift me into a boat, truck, and gondola, or even wiggle me into a wet suit! Although I would get frustrated by the things that fell through the cracks because it was now one, rather than two, trying to get things done, I had to let it go. Steve always maintained his "we can deal with it" attitude.

"Nobody trips over mountains.
It is the small pebble that causes you to stumble.
Pass all the pebbles in your path and
you will find you have crossed the mountain."
~ Author Unknown

Seeing that I am now doing most of the sports I did before the crash, my friends sometimes forget that I cannot walk. I love it when they forget, because it proves that, for them, my new situation is the "new normal" and I CAN STILL DO IT!

Chapter 6
Testing Extreme Measures

**With the hope of more accelerated improvement
and the dream of walking again,
I tried stem-cell treatments.**

In 2012, I decided to take a chance on the evolving medicine of stem-cell treatments. I knew that spinal injury stem-cell trials were very new in the United States, and that other countries had been getting good results. Also, I had learned that stem-cell treatments used in horses had been successful—that was good enough for me! Rather than jump in full bore, however, I decided to try a simpler treatment first. I went to the Asian Stem Cell Institute in Arizona, where they extracted stem cells from my own adipose (fat) and injected them near my injury site. My body's response was good, so I decided to get the next level of treatment at the Stem Cell Institute in Panama City, Panama. I was attracted to Panama because it had American-trained doctors located in a cosmopolitan city. Plus, I could speak Spanish, having studied it in high school and practiced whenever I could. Besides, it would be a new, highly recommended travel place to visit for Steve and me.

We were told that we would have to spend a month for my first round of treatments—injections, rest, and physical therapy—so we rented a condo in town. We were so happy to find that it had a bathroom with a walk-in shower. With minor adjustments, Steve made the place work for my wheelchair needs, like removing the bathroom door so my wheelchair would fit through. We even had a view of the ocean and the marina! Between treatments, we were quite adventurous, having reconfigured my wheelchair's tires with mountain-bike tires for the rougher terrains and the broken or missing sidewalks in Panama City.

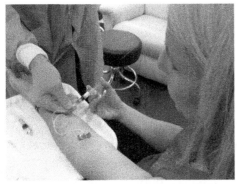

The initial treatment plan was to extract my own stem cells and grow them. Then, I would receive a number of injections of my own stem cells alternating with umbilical-cord stem cells. Every weekday morning, I would have physical therapy, and three days a week the workout would be followed by injections. In order to help teach the cells what to do, I would do vigorous physical therapy.

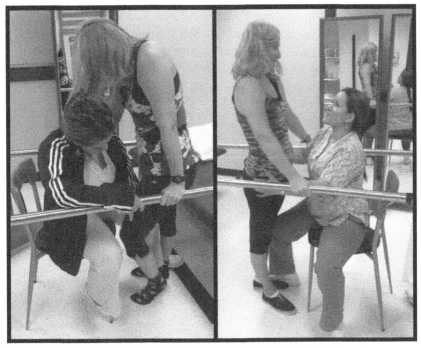

Many hours of rehab

While waiting for my own cells to multiply, I fell into a workout routine. My physical therapist, Joclyn, had me do exercises like getting on my hands and knees, standing/walking in the parallel bars, or throwing a ball while sitting. I would also work my legs on the exercise ball, sort of like horseback riding. The exercises sounded simple, but they were very hard for me. It sometimes took everything that I had, but it was worth the effort because I got more proficient and stronger. Before the trip to Panama, I had taken three funky steps with my left leg at Dr. Zhu's office, and at home, I had taken five steps on the same side. To my surprise, on this trip, under Joclyn's watchful spotting and training, I took twenty actual steps with my left leg, and—for the first time ever—I took about five actual steps with my right leg. Another miraculous day!

The physical therapy was five days each week for the four weeks I was there. On the days without injections we would go exploring, while on injection days we would go to lunch. Between therapy and the injections, we had time for lunch at the most amazing restaurants. The food was delicious and cheap, enjoying different international cuisines. Surprisingly, the hardest cuisine to find was Panamanian food. We searched for the delicious food and found that locals ate it at home, not in restaurants. After lunch, I had to face the dreaded needles—how I hated them since it was the pain of needle sticks! A few of the times, as soon as the doctor stuck a needle into the lumbar area, I could feel tingling from the top of both legs all the way down to my feet. I

immediately felt good after the IV. However, I'd have to rest afterwards for the entire afternoon, and some days I was in more pain than others.

When I wasn't getting my treatments, Steve and I took advantage of this Pacific Coast paradise. We rolled around the city seeing the native historical sites. On one of our weekends, we even rented a car and went to a small, private resort called Otro de Lado on the Caribbean side of the country. No other tourists were there, and we enjoyed an amazing meal and then went kayaking in the ocean around the island. A few of the resort workers followed us in a flat boat, carrying water and snacks for us. As we kayaked from one bay to another, I realized I was using both my legs to keep steady. When we got to the beach at the turnaround point, we swam. The crew expected us to ride back in their boat, but we paddled ourselves back to the resort in the kayak. What a thrill to be so active in such a beautiful place. Before we returned to Panama City, we enjoyed another fresh caught seafood meal.

All of the adventures, including off-roading on the crumpled sidewalks and swimming in the pool, were made possible by Steve continuing to be my hero, occasionally lifting me when necessary to preserve our earlier lifestyle. I did as much as I could, but many times I was healing from the injections and not quite as mobile.

The month went by fast and the day before we left Panama, I was feeling strong, doing leg exercises during my PT routine. The PT room had a TV, and I watched the Olympics, which also spurred me on. As tired as I was from my workout, it was my time to stand in the parallel bars and try to walk. To my amazement, I walked four times up and back in the bars, advancing both legs without any help. For me, that was miraculous. I was so determined to work hard that the staff there called me *furiousa* (ferocious). They also called me, "just one more," since I always pushed past when I thought I was done. Joclyn knew to let me go one more time even when I was tired. It was so amazing to walk upright!

It was time for my last injection before I returned home. I was told that I would start seeing results in a minimum of six weeks as the nerves regenerated. It was highly recommended to keep up the physical therapy in order to help the stem cells do their work. These unmarked baby stem cells had to be taught what to do. To continue the improvement and get the best result, we needed to go back for a second round of injections in about six months.

We traveled back to Panama in January 2013—this time for only two weeks. As before, I was getting physical therapy every morning and injections every other day, in the afternoons. Unlike before, I was in better shape, but my movement didn't seem to be improving. The treatments were still wiping me out, even though I was making sure that I rested after each injection. Sometimes, when I got the injections, I had the sensation of fluid running down my left leg and into my groin. While it hurt sometimes, most of the time it was just a strange feeling, yet not painful.

On a weekend for one of our excursions to the Pacific side of the coastline, we met a fellow who had multiple sclerosis and could only lie flat before he had stem-cell treatments. Afterward, he could golf and  swim. He had his life back! After the start of the second week, we hired a taxi to go to the Canal in between IV treatments. That was fun, because on our previous trip we had boarded a ship going through the locks, but we couldn't see much because we had to be on the lowest deck to accommodate my wheel-chair. We also snuck in a day trip back to the Caribbean side to our favorite resort to relax, kayak, and swim.

This time around, the treatments were taking a lot out of me. Before this second trip to Panama, I had been walking up and back twenty times in the parallel bars at Dr. Zhu's office. It was so exciting to be getting cardio and doing that much walking. I even walked several times with just a walker. For safety, the PT had to watch my knees so they wouldn't buckle. To my surprise, on this Panamanian trip, under Joclyn's continual spotting, I could stand all by myself without any support and I walked easily in her parallel bars.

When we got back to California, I didn't feel well, though; I had flu-like symptoms, and Steve thought it was just a stiff neck and soreness from the flight home. Since I had a bad feeling about it, and as an EMT, I did a medical test on myself by moving my neck to my chest. Yes, I had the specific symptom of spinal meningitis called nuchal rigidity, and it was confirmed with a spinal tap; then I was admitted to Los Gatos Community Hospital on my thirty-year wedding anniversary.

The intense doses of antibiotics they gave me helped, but the spinal and infectious-disease doctors were still worried that I might need spinal surgery to remove the abscess. Spinal meningitis can be fatal, so I made sure that I did the right things. The doctors were also concerned that the meningitis can lay dormant around the metal plates at the two spinal fusion sites and the ankle. Therefore, aggressive and extensive treatment was mandated. At least, I did not need surgery, since I responded well to ten days of treatment in the hospital. I even found parallel bars to walk in, albeit groggily. Finally, I got released from the hospital with six weeks of IV antibiotics that Steve would administer through a PIC-line. I was beginning to feel that I could be a physical therapist or a doctor, with all of the knowledge I was gaining combined with all my schooling and training. Because of the PIC-line, I couldn't take Lindsay to Mexico for her high-school graduation present that we had previously scheduled. My parents stepped in, thank goodness, and took her to Mexico for us. Once the PIC-line came out, I stayed on antibiotics for a year before being cleared. Being told that I could go off the antibiotics was such great news, since I was originally told that I would have to be on them for life.

The spinal meningitis really set me back: I found I couldn't stand for long without help, because one of my knees would usually buckle instead of locking. Also, I found out that the antibiotics also killed off the stem-cell treatments, resetting my progress back to square one. Unfortunately, spinal meningitis stays with you for life! At least I survived, and I planned on doing the hard work to build my muscles back up.

Steve and I had always liked to travel, so we were lucky my stem-cell treatments were in Panama, both times. Since we had both been able to retire from our jobs around the age of forty (though I continued to go in and out of my real estate career), our relative freedom and family support system also enabled us to try many avenues to help with the recovery from the crash.

Chapter 7
The Draw of Work

Real estate is in my DNA.
and I wanted to contribute again to my profession.

Although I was still healing after the crash, Steve and I got asked to teach Advanced First Aid at several different companies. It was surprising to me how well I could demonstrate medical skills despite my new condition. Each class would ask questions and the creative answers that I would present were from all the experience that I had from ski patrol and teaching for Industrial Emergency Council (IEC). I found that the teaching was extra stimulating since we were interacting with intellectual groups of employees at these high-tech companies.

Two years after my injury, Jeff, a former competitor in the real estate business asked me if I wanted to help him continue to build his strong office at Alain Pinel Realtors (APR) in Los Gatos. I had already had a very successful career as a Senior Vice President at Cornish and Carey/Coldwell Banker before the crash, overseeing the entire Silicon Valley Region as well as leading/managing five different offices in Santa Clara County. While I was always a leader in sales, I liked managing offices and mentoring sales teams. Real estate sales, for me, was very rewarding to help people fulfill their real estate dreams whether selling or buying a home. (I even was the top agent in my large office my first full year in the business.)

What Jeff offered was the best opportunity for me at this time: to work part-time and to help him strengthen APR's office. APR was a similar family, yet a large independent company like Cornish and Carey was. I started right away, doing special projects, helping with office meetings, and working with the agents to help build their business. My experience of being a top agent and a top managing broker earlier in my career gave me credibility and knowledge about how to be successful. I knew the ins and outs of the profession!

It was great to be going back to work; I hadn't realized how much I missed real estate. Looking back, I understood how so many of the things I did throughout my life contributed to my success in this field. I started babysitting young. My dad gave me a job when I was starting high school managing the horse stables on our property. At the same time, I waitressed in high school and all through college. And, as an Alpha Phi sorority sister, I planned and directed recruiting and many social events as the rush chairman. Right out of college, I had worked at a chemical distributor doing inside sales and working as their chemical lab technician. Then, while Steve and I lived in Hawaii after we were first married (he was stationed on Oahu in the Army), I worked in sales and soon after became the sales manager for an elite business health club. All of these positions required managing and working with the public while problem solving. For me, real estate is helping families make one of the most important decisions in their life—choosing a home or selling one—and was the ultimate in customer service.

As fabulous as this business opportunity was, I had to deal with new challenges from my paralysis. To get to work, I had to bring my wheelchair with me in a car modified with hand controls. There were two ways that I could manage the chair: One was with help, and the other was by myself. Sometimes, Steve would put the chair into the back of the car and follow me to work to get it out. Other times, someone at the office would come out of the building and pull the chair out of the back of my car so that I could get in the wheelchair. I had to plan if I would have someone to help me in and out. One time, I had another challenge I hadn't considered. Steve put my chair in the back of my car and off I went to work. A few miles past home, I stopped at a stop sign and for some reason looked in my review mirror. I am not sure why, with the chair I couldn't see out the back. Well, thankfully I did, my hatchback door was open and I couldn't get out and close it. "Oh my, what could I do; no one is around and my chair could go flying out," I thought. I carefully drove a little further and spotted a woman carrying a plateful of cookies crossing the street. I stopped and begged her to close the trunk. Crisis adverted. Soon after, I got an updated Subaru Outback which has an automated push-button on the dash so that I can close the back. It has come in handy a number of times already.

If I wasn't sure that I would have help, I would load the chair myself. Here was the routine: Transfer from my wheelchair into the driver's seat, making sure that I had pulled the chair right up to the door opening. The door had to be open as wide as possible to fit the chair and allow me to transfer. Once in the car, I would have to take off the chair's seat cushion, and then each wheel, and place them in the back seat of the car. Then, I would have to make sure that my car seat was all the way back, fold the back of the wheelchair down, pull up the chair frame, and drag it over my lap and chest without hitting the steering wheel, placing it in the passenger seat. Many times, I would get wheel marks on the ceiling of my car from the chair's little front wheels as I moved the frame upside down over my lap. I laid beach towels across my lap so as not to ruin my clothing and protect the car and another towel went on the center console. When I arrived at my destination, I had to do the same procedure in reverse. Eventually, I accomplished this entire procedure in three minutes, but I had to allow this extra time for any meetings or events that I went to. That was three minutes on both sides; I had to be well planned.

There were three other big challenges that I had to deal with daily. The easiest issue was picking out my clothes and getting dressed. Then comes using the bathroom. The most challenging is dealing with daily pain.

The bathroom at my work is a perfect ADA (American with Disabilities Act) set-up, but not all bathrooms that I needed to use were. Sadly, even when they were supposedly ADA-compliant, they weren't designed for a wheelchair user. Many times, the stall wasn't wide enough for the wheelchair to fit in or the sink was in the way. One of my pet peeves was when a bathroom had a trash can that had a foot-operated cover. Really, I wished that I could open the can with my foot. These challenges were so hard for me, especially in the beginning, because I had what was called a spastic bladder, so I couldn't hold much volume. For someone who was used to drinking a lot of water, it was difficult to drink even a standard amount without having to go all the time. Limiting what I drank and avoiding caffeine or alcohol, I would try to make it to three hours between trips to the bathroom. I had even less bladder control when I had a UTI (Urinary Tract Infection) or was ill. Eventually the planning got easier since we found medicines that relaxed my bladder, and I had much more control. And I was lucky that I usually had the sensation of having to go, just like people who are not paralyzed do. That was a relief. I still had the inconvenience of having to monitor everything I drank and watery foods that I ate, since the volume changed the timing. This is not to mention how difficult salty foods complicated the timing. It was easiest to be dehydrated when I was intensely involved in work or with colleagues and clients. Many times, the risk outweighed the benefits of drinking that delicious coffee. Two of the things other paraplegics and I talk about are our inability to walk and our toileting needs. We agree that if we had to choose between the two, we would choose to use the bathroom like everyone else. We have to really pay attention to timing and fluid intake to prevent "accidents" that can be quite embarrassing.

The other big challenge was dealing with the pain. The longer I sat, the more pain I had. Although I found solutions to managing the pain, they didn't always help. Often, I had to work through the pain or just go home and lie down. And, some days the pain just intensified as the day went on, no matter what I was doing. Exercise was my favorite type of pain relief, but I was limited with exercise when I was working. Distraction ended up being the easiest form of relief. Whether I was teaching or ingrained in a problem-solving mission, my pain level dropped or temporarily went away.

For my type of business, it was typical to run into the office to pick up something or make a call. However, "running in" wasn't possible, so I had to allow more time. By the time I took my chair out of the car and put it back in, I had used up a lot of effort and, more importantly, time. For the effort, I had to add on ten more minutes. If I was more patient, that time would be nothing. When it rained, it became even more of a problem. I had to roll up to the car, put my computer and paperwork in, then myself, and then the chair. By the time I was done, I was soaked. An umbrella didn't work, because I had to use both hands to push my wheelchair. I even tried someone pushing me while I held the umbrella, but would keep hitting my helper in the face with the umbrella. There are so many details like this that people with paralysis have to deal with.

Even making and then transporting coffee or tea was a challenge. Though I learned how to make it myself in our kitchen at home, making it in the office was more difficult, because I had to reach the supplies and then get it back to my own office while using both my hands to roll my chair. I worked out a system like a canoeist: paddling on one side (wheeling) and then the other, holding the thermos cup in the opposite hand and then moving the cup to the other side. Of course, an open cup did not work. I would get more liquid all over me than what stayed in the cup.

As a professional, it was a good thing suits were my uniform because I couldn't wear dresses: They were too hard to get right while sitting in my chair as well as managing bathroom breaks. While choosing jackets was easy, deciding on pants was not: I had enough sensation in my butt to hate the seams and extra fabric of pockets or even flaps. As broad as I hope to make it, the styling was very limited. When low-waisted pants came into style, it was even more of a problem, since I was uncomfortable wearing them when I sat. They were definitely designed for standing.

Despite all of these challenges, I was happy to be working and contributing again. I had always been a good planner, but with my new

life, I had to be even better with time management. As an entrepreneur in a business where flexibility was a must, I really had to be strong with my scheduling. My job at Alain Pinel Realtors was rewarding, because I created and implemented trainings, tours, coaching, and special events for our agents.

And in 2013, our son TJ became a Realtor in our office. He had worked in construction before getting his college degree, a B.S. in

My son TJ working with me

business. What a reward it was to mentor him, passing along my knowledge and practical advice. During the same year, I also became a district chair for the Los Gatos / Saratoga district of the Silicon Valley Association of Realtors (SILVAR) and a member of the board of directors of the California Association of Realtors (C.A.R.). With Steve's assistance, I traveled to Monterey, Sacramento, and Long Beach on C.A.R. business focused on protecting private home ownership rights.

At APR, I was able to grow in my knowledge of selling and mentoring. The business continues to change, and I like being on the cutting edge. *I CAN STILL DO IT!* In 2014, I became a director at-large for SILVAR and the next year became the president-elect for 2015. I enjoyed leading this organization of about 5,000 members of Realtors and Affiliates.

During my time as president-elect, I made seven trips for C.A.R. and the National Association of Realtors (NAR) —among them, Chicago, Washington, D. C., and Portland. Steve and I fit in visits with family and friends along the way, enjoying our ability to mix business with pleasure. My work life accelerated the next year when I became President of SILVAR. Life was very full. One of my greatest experiences was the advocacy work we did in Sacramento and Washington, D. C. to protect homeowners' property rights.

One of the hardest parts in Real Estate was that there was always a few friends or potential clients who would do business with other people. As a people pleaser, I knew that I would do the best job for agents or clients whether it was in mentoring them, selling their home for the best value or finding the right property. I had to get over myself since I did miss opportunities. Sometimes being in the wheelchair went against me. It was upsetting at first, and then I realized that whether I was able-bodied or in a chair, I wasn't going to get to work with everyone. Then I would think of my motto, "making a difference in peoples' lives," which drives me to do the absolute best for my clients.

"To give real service, you must add something which cannot be bought or measured with money, and that is sincerity and integrity."
~ Douglas Adams

When Lindsay joined my company, Alain Pinel Realtors, in 2016, it was icing on the cake for me. Not only was I helping to manage the office, but also, I had the chance to mentor two of my children in a profession I loved.

As SILVAR President, with my daughter Lindsay

Marketing one of my real estate listings in Los Gatos

Chapter 8
Relearning Sports Adaptively

Active and athletic before the crash,
I was determined to play sports again—
whatever it took!

My life was always very active, constantly moving since I couldn't sit still; I liked participating in most every sport. Since I wasn't a good spectator, I wasn't about to let a life-changing experience stop me. Just because I didn't have use of my legs didn't mean that I had to sit around and watch the world go by. I was determined to continue to live my life to the fullest. With training, I found out that I could do most of the sports I did earlier—adaptively.

The first sport that I got involved in after the crash was swimming. Although I could swim well using my arms, without the use of my legs I wasn't the racer that I used to be in triathlons. I moved through the water slowly, but I did make it from one side of the pool to the other. My legs helped keep my balance and I was able to do several different strokes. I also found that I had to breathe more often, since my punctured lung didn't allow me to hold large amounts of air. But swimming helped me safely transition to other water sports, like body surfing, snorkeling, sailing, waterskiing, and kayaking.

Swimming and body surfing were very similar, but I loved being in the open water riding a wave. Every chance I got to be in a warm water ocean, Steve would get me in the water and I would swim out to the waves. By the time I made it to the surf, Steve was by my side. We would race to catch the wave and see who could ride it longer. I must have been more buoyant because I would finish slightly ahead.

Little did I realize that all that happened earlier in my life helped set me up for adaptive sports. Luckily, like my father who retired at forty, I had decided to take an early retirement, at age forty-three. My husband was retiring, too, and really encouraged me to do so, to help him and also have more time for family, sports, and travel. My parents had a cabin at Lake Tahoe, and before the crash we could canoe, sail, swim, water ski, and windsurf on the lake and bicycle around the lake. In the winter, we would snow ski or snow board at the nearby ski resorts. I also became involved in all of my kids' sports, whether coaching girls' recreational and then competitive soccer, or managing Andrew's Pop Warner football team, or coaching TJ's competitive soccer team.

Steve and I both took the Emergency Medical Technician (EMT) and Wilderness Emergency Medical Technician training at a local community college. It would stand me in good stead immediately after the crash, for I knew to stay still until my injuries were assessed. And the training led to many volunteer and paid opportunities during my relatively short retirement. (I couldn't stay away from real estate very long.) Steve and I joined the Disaster Aid Response Team (DART) in Los Gatos, the First Aid Support Team (FAST)) with the American Red Cross, the Ski Patrol at Northstar California, and I.E.C. (Industrial Emergency Council).

We took ropes rescue courses in Belize as well as an advanced course on rope rescue in our county to use to teach our tech rescue team in DART, where we also joined the bike, ATV, and dive teams. To stay current with diving, we continued to dive all over the world. What a time we had!

Soon after I was released from the hospital, I jumped back into my role as a ski patrol instructor, but I didn't start learning to ski until a year later. While I coached candidates on all aspects of patrolling, my favorite was on-the-hill toboggan rescues, where I could sit in a sled or toboggan to get down the hills. But I really wanted to ski myself. On the advice of my friend Sharon, I finally turned to an expert adaptive ski instructor at Alpine Ski Resort. Little did I know that it would be as challenging to learn adaptive skiing as it was to learn the sport in the first place!

To learn skiing, the Alpine Team fitted me into a monoski that included an adaptive system with a shock absorber and a bucket to sit in. Since this bucket would act like my boots, it had to fit tightly. I found it very difficult to transfer and then settle into the right position in the "boot." My instructor, Bill Bowness, was also a paraplegic, and he taught me how to ski on flat snow with the monoski and—just as important— how to get around in the snow using my wheelchair. He probably laughed when he saw how I tried to "motorcycle" the monoski. I would lean or bank for a turn as if I were on my motorcycle. But every time I did this, I fell over. He taught me how to use my hips to carve and my arms as the fulcrum for the turning angles. On my second day, another instructor, Dave, controlled my speed with a piece of webbing, allowing me to make turns and not worry about going too fast.

My progress on the slopes was slower than I expected, though. I thought that all of my previous skiing experience would accelerate my learning process, but working with a monoski was like learning to ski all over again. Fortunately, my instructors knew I needed a challenge and took me on more aggressive slopes beyond the beginner slopes as soon as they thought I was ready.

In the winter of 2012–13, I got my own monoski for Christmas. Bill helped me set it up, but still, the only runs I took were during my ski patrol stints and on the flat areas. The following season, my friend Nate, also an adaptive skier and racer, helped me with a few more tips. He advised that I should focus on looking down-hill and leaning forward, simply moving with my hips. I discovered that it was harder skiing on the flats than skiing on more aggressive slopes fol-lowing the fall line. Nate was a good role model because he was faster than many of the able-bodied ski patrollers, and these patrollers told me that they were impressed with how well he navigated the slopes.

The next year, we drove to Breckenridge, Colorado, for their adaptive ski program. I had a great time learning how to ski on steeper bunny slopes, mainly because I didn't get hurt when I fell over since the snow was so soft. Many times when I fell, I did cartwheels on the slope, hitting my head. Even though "ringing my bell" wasn't a good thing, I kept on skiing and finally could call myself a solid beginner.

During the 2015–2016 season, while ski patrolling at Northstar, I received a "standing ovation" from a line of ski patrollers as I skied past. I was amazed that I didn't fall and thrilled to have the team be so supportive of me. Near the end of the season, I was invited to a Paralympics' ski camp at Achieve Tahoe at Alpine Meadows, where I received instruction from two Paralympic gold medalists. They told me that the ski I was using wasn't working well for me (Ha! Blame it on the equipment), but I also learned that I was bringing my arms in too close when I started my turn. Because of this training, I was even able to tackle more difficult slopes and fulfilled a dream by helping to "close" Northstar as a patroller on my last day of the season.

Later that year, after the end of the Northstar season, Steve and I went to Mammoth and spent two days trying out three different monoskis. I couldn't decide which ski worked the best for me, so I purchased the least expensive one. The following season on this new ski system while in a lesson, I found out that besides my adaptive ski system, I really should replace the actual ski that completed the system. And two companies donated new skis to me: one was for powder and the other for all-mountain skiing. What a difference they made! At the end of the season, I could call myself a solid intermediate skier and discovered that *I CAN STILL DO IT!* I will continue practicing; I want to get back up to the advanced level, although I am told that mogul skiing is out.

My snow ski coach (Bill) is also a national champion adaptive water skier, and he encouraged me to get back in the water, using a fat ski with a "cage" for sitting in. During the summer, I went to the disabled sports program in Sacramento and learned adaptive waterskiing on a tiny lake (pond). Water skiing was more natural for me; in fact, I felt as though I was skiing as an able-bodied person on the water, the first time. Skiing was exhilarating and refreshing.

I eventually went to Mississippi to get instruction on a private water ski lake at Bill's home. Steve and I drove there in our RV and stayed on Bill's property. The challenge of water skiing was learning how to get into the ski myself without help. At first, when I fell and came out of the ski, I had to pull against the boat and rope to pop in. I got better under Bill's tutelage and even started running buoys on his slalom course. Ironically,

I ran the course about as well as I did when I could able-body ski (which then wasn't that great). Upon returning home, I ordered a water ski that I could use.

Receiving great water ski lessons on the private lake in Mississippi.

The best place to water ski near our home is Calero Reservoir. In the fall, there is little wind, and the water is beautifully flat. Although I was able to hold an edge in my turn, I couldn't seem to keep the edge across the wake. I was hoping that with a tuned-up ski I would be able to do it. Because I skied hard and had feeling in the bottom of my feet, I had to wear water shoes to be comfortable. I couldn't tell you how many shoes I have donated to that lake! Since we always needed a third person in the ski boat, we would take friends or family along. Our son Andrew enjoyed using my adaptive ski as well as his slalom one. What fun it was to join in my family's activities and not be a bystander.

I also got out kayaking. After the crash, Steve found a used, two-seater one—good for travel, because it was foldable. We had tested my ability to kayak as a paraplegic in Alaska, the Caribbean, and San Diego, but with our own kayak we could go out more regularly at Tahoe or lakes near our home. Steve would set up the kayak at the dock, lower me into the kayak from it, then jump in and push off. (Luckily, he was as agile as he was!) We were moving, paddling hard while looking at places where we could ride horses. I was pleased by how synchronized we became in our strokes. I was no longer sliding down with every stroke, as I had during my early days. Steve had installed a footrest to help me stay put. Getting out of this foldable kayak was more complicated than getting in, though. My hips kept getting caught on the curved sides of the boat, and Steve had to wrestle me out.

Always up for a new challenge, I was prompted to learn how to shoot skeet by TJ. I soon discovered how tough it is to hit a moving target, especially from a wheelchair. I had to use a shotgun that didn't have a lot of kick or it would dump me backwards in the chair. Soon after this practice, TJ got me a compound bow for Christmas and taught me the best hold, since I couldn't offset the shots with my stance. He set up targets at our home, and I have to admit I became a good shot. It was so much fun to try new sports!

All-terrain vehicles (ATVs) were another fun "sport" to try. Although I used to ride in those with manual transmissions, now I could run them if they had automatic transmissions. When I first was learning, Andrew or TJ would ride with me on a used one we bought. It was fun to ride fast and furious up hills and around corners on our property. Even our horse, Josie, became desensitized as I arrived via ATV with her carrots. Over time, my body core got strong enough that I could ride the ATV in our town's annual holiday parade for the Disaster Aid Response Team. Doing so became a family tradition.

Probably the sport that I do most consistently is horseback riding. I ride two or three times a week when the weather allows, and I recognize how lucky I am because we can ride right from our property or trailer the horses to several beautiful parks nearby. The best part of riding so often is the effect it has on strengthening my core, arms, and legs. Riding can also greatly reduce my pain, at least for several hours after the ride. To balance, I move around on the saddle a lot, pushing down with my legs, since I haven't been able to squeeze my legs yet. And I use the saddle horn to counter balance the reins and hold on!

Riding at Salinas River Beach on the Pacific Ocean

One day, a friend that I rode with a lot took off after we went through the initial trail gate. I was right behind her. Suddenly, she stopped and apologized. She had forgotten that I was a disabled rider. I loved it, because my old self loved speed—safe speed. Then, I would ride fast through the hills. I am proud to say, after these years of practice as a paraplegic rider, my horse and I can now go up and down stairs, on the beach, through the trees, across rivers, and up and down hills on horseback. Since the most common riding I did was walking or gaiting on a single track or wider trails, the first time I galloped up a hill I was shocked. I honestly didn't think that was something that I could do in my new adaptive life, but *I CAN STILL DO IT!*

My biggest reward is riding on the beach. Salinas River Beach isn't too far away and allows horses. Although our horses aren't very comfortable by the crashing waves, at least they will let us guide them on the wet sand. I am still working them to get into the water. Riding along the beach is so beautiful and gives me serenity. However, always thinking of the horses, one time we couldn't ride on the beach because there were school children out running on the beach. Their noise was making the horses too upset. A friend once told me that although horses have a brain, they are animals and spook easily.

Again, Steve makes it possible. He saddles the horses and gets me on by himself, unless we have the luxury of another person to help stand me up and load me. The hardest part is when I have to get off on the trail or when I fall off; thank goodness this is seldom. Then, I need help to remount from the ground. But we have developed a good system for this. At the finish of our rides, the horses love spying the wheelchair because they know that treats are soon to follow.

Class 3 white water rafting in Washington with Paul Cardus and Steve

Sports are an important part of my life. Besides the physical therapy role they play, they allow me to enjoy physical exercise with friends and family. And they allow me to exercise my competitive nature, if only with myself. While engaging in sports, I feel more like "my old self" and healthy.

Chapter 9
Paraplegic Black Belt

With instructors, I adapt Traditional Martial Arts to match my body.

Before the crash, Steve and I were very involved with our three children. At one time, the whole family was enrolled in Martial Arts. The Tae Kwon Do studio was in town, and we worked hard learning the art. Lindsay, being too little, started after the boys had moved up several belt levels, moving from white to yellow to green belt. All three kids gained the confidence and discipline that martial arts teaches. For TJ and Andrew, martial arts helped them be more focused and accomplished in their other sports, especially soccer. Lindsay and Steve just trained for fun, whereas I did it for me. As a Senior Vice President/Regional Manager, I needed the training for exercise and stress relief. The extra benefits came from the lessons I learned, which were useful when I taught business and leadership subjects. For all of us, the discipline and the physical training were awesome; and for me at each of my tests, I would learn to overcome a mental challenge as a life lesson.

One of the lessons that I learned was focus. Whatever you focus on you will attain. Make sure you focus on the right things. In a test for a lower level belt, I had to break a board with an axe kick. I brought my straight leg up and broke the board in half. I was so proud! But the instructor picked up the larger of the two halves and held it for me to break. I had never done this before and psyched myself up. All I could see were his fingers holding the board. I thought, "I can do this; just do it." I brought my leg up and powered through the kick. Guess what? I slammed his fingers. We both regained composure and then I focused on the target, the center of the board, did a strong axe kick, and the board broke in half. Whatever you truly focus on, you will get. Make sure that you focus on the right target.

In my Tae Kwon Do studio, I had the opportunity to work with many different weapons like the staff, Sai, and sticks as well as work in Qigong and Kendo (sword art). This training was differentiated at each belt level and helped me push to become strong at all the forms and techniques that I had to learn. The only real setback that I had to overcome occurred when I was training for my black belt. We were out at a local field performing flying sidekicks; and when I came down on the wet grass, I rolled my ankle. I had to have a fellow student and friend drive me home because I couldn't work my car's clutch. Luckily, my sprained ankle healed in time for the test. I was presented with my first-degree black belt. It really demonstrates that "a black belt is a white belt that never quit." Ultimately, I became an instructor while also practicing and finishing my first martial arts training in Tae Kwon Do as a second-degree black belt.

Even after the rest of the family quit training, Lindsay and I transitioned to the Japanese-Hawaiian art of Kenpo Jujitsu at Pacific Coast Academy (PCA). In fact, the head of the art, Shihan Russ Rhodes, had been ranked in a number of different arts and included the techniques and philosophies in his classes. Not only did I learn the patterns, but I also learned what I was doing and why. With this new understanding, I improved quickly. These arts were so much more elaborate yet worked very succinctly. Much of the training required a partner to help with the learning and to make sure the techniques would work for self-defense.

I found it so rewarding teaching classes to adults at the Tae Kwon Do studio that I knew I missed instructing. Shihan spent two months getting me up to speed with Kenpo and then I started teaching the children. These kids seemed to appreciate the training even more than the adults I had taught at the other studio. And, the instruction helped me understand all the Kenpo moves, since I had to break each one down in order to teach them. Then when I went to my adult classes I could focus more on learning jujitsu.

Taking my time to learn, I had an appreciation for this jujitsu art since the moves taught real self-defense. Jujitsu consisted of many techniques including throws and falls. As I got better, I learned the tsutemi fall. Since I threw my partner, he would throw and I would have to fall. So, I worked the fall, spreading the energy down my body. I could take the fall when I was thrown, but I struggled with the practice of throwing myself. It seemed if I just touched someone else's finger, I could do this flip-like fall.

But it was ugly if I did it just myself in the air. I tried to perfect it while I continued my training. I was learning so many different pieces of the arts and I even learned how to grapple. All of the techniques that I learned and applied gave me the knowledge of how to defend myself from the ground as well as from a standing position, which are very important for women to know. Lindsay was strong in the art but quit when she got into middle school; as a typical teenager, she focused on other things.

Steve joined me in learning the sword art while I spent the majority of my training time in Kenpo Jujitsu and Jujitsu. We started with Shinkendo but the master instructor evidentially found a more inclusive art. The second art that we learned was Toyama Ryu, the Japanese Military Sword Art. It was so amazing working with an ancient sword as I learned how the Japanese Samurai moved. I even practiced my art wielding the sword on wet tatami mats. During one of my tests, the instructor asked me to make as many cuts as I could before the mat fell. I positioned myself, then lifted my sword over my head, and dropped the sword down making a beautiful diagonal cut. In rapid succession, I did it four more times. I even surprised myself that I made five cuts before the mat and pieces fell to the ground.

For me, jujitsu was the most difficult martial art to learn since it was very different learning to throw, roll, and fall. Throwing a big guy was challenging because I had to throw him using good technique. I would walk him to change his balance, turn into him, get my body correctly under him, and then throw him. Then, he would get to return the practice—thankfully. I learned to fall spreading the energy throughout my body, because I used the falling discipline as a paraplegic. One of the guys that I trained with was very tall, Rob. He would move me, turn, and then have to bend low to throw me over his shoulder. I learned how to safely land from a tall throw. This training benefited me in my early horseback riding days when I came off the horse. I landed well finding it was an easier fall than coming out of my wheelchair when the little wheels would catch.

After the crash, though, I truly thought I was done with this practice in my life. I thought, "How can I move and do Martial Arts in a wheelchair? My legs won't kick and how could I stand and throw? And, there are certain moves I could do with my sword but other ones would be foolish for me to try." I really missed my karate family and I stopped by the studio one day, about a year after the accident. The master at my studio, Shihan, invited me to train, and he adapted many Kenpo Jujitsu techniques for me to continue my practice. Although I couldn't do falls or kicks, there was still a lot of Kenpo Jujitsu, Jujitsu, and Escrima that I could do. We incorporated hand drills, self- defense moves, and Escrima into a program for the sitting position. There are even throwing techniques that I can do. It was so wonderful to take an art that was for the able-bodied and make it work for paraplegics. Self-defense knowledge is even more important for people in wheel chairs. After a couple of years, I was honored to be tested and then presented with my second degree in Kenpo Jujitsu in my wheelchair, and now I am training for my third-degree black belt.

Excited to be invited back to adapt the arts

My passion for Safety and Self-Defense for Realtors allowed me to use my martial arts knowledge to continue teaching programs both for my office and the Silicon Valley Association of Realtors. We taught both women and men how to be aware of the dangerous signs and how to protect themselves at open houses or showing properties. Two of the classes that we held for SILVAR included my talented partner Alex Franckx and a magnificent sixth-degree black belt, Carla Bunch. She demon-strated all the movements that I couldn't. She is an amazing jujitsu sensei, and we were lucky to have her teach with us. We enjoyed working together and I learned from her.

With her encouragement, Carla recommended that I compete in the Self-Defense category in a Jujitsu tournament. I had never competed before, let alone on an international level; so with my partner Alex and Shihan, we came up with five dramatic wheelchair self-defenses. It took a lot of work, but it was so much fun knowing that I could respond to an attacker. The day came and I won a gold medal in my wheelchair. Just as rewarding, I was told by spectators that I had the cleanest techniques of the many other competitors.

Escrima (sticks) training

Posing with escrima sticks

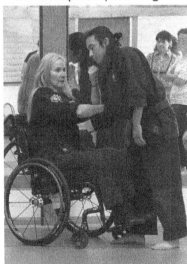

Demonstrating an upper cut

Showing a choke

Even more surprising and humbling to me was that I got invited to a celebration down in Los Angeles by Dr. Marc Stoner, a high ranking martial artist. There I was inducted into the Legends of Martial Arts Hall of Fame with the "Extraordinary Achievements in the Martial Arts" Awards. Famous Actors and Grandmasters were presenters and had been previously included in this group. Dr. Marc told the audience why I was being inducted and Grandmaster Cynthia Rothrock, my martial arts idol, presented the plaque. To receive a standing ovation from all these amazing leaders put tears in my eyes. As an outstanding first, I was inspired to build on my training and focus on the wheelchair art. It is important to me to have a true effective Martial Art for people in wheelchairs!

Award was presented to me by Grand Master/Actress
Cynthia Rothrock and Master Eric Kovalski

Our wheelchair art continues to build with functional techniques. Not only is my own fabulous training building with Shihan Russ, but also, I have been blessed with learning other arts. Dr. Marc invited both Steve and me to train with him in small circles with Sensei Bob Hodge. Building on the focused joint-lock training, Sifu Mark Gerry is teaching me nerve strikes. His speed is amazingly fast. I will need to continually practice to even be half as fast. Being in a chair, I found that I lose the power driven from my hips that I had in a fighting (standing) stance. Specific localized and explosive strikes are critical for my self-defense.

At a medical conference that we were invited to, we learned a lot about medical healing and other martial arts. We were surrounded by doctors and famous actors/Grandmaster martial artists from all different types of arts. One evening a group of us went out to dinner. While waiting for the check, the Grandmaster and student of Ip Man came over and asked me if I wanted to learn Wing Chun. Of course, I said yes, although I didn't know the art at all. A very tactile and flowing art, Sifu Samuel Kwok taught me the basics. A fist would come at my face. Immediately I would block the punch with one hand and deliver a punch with the other hand. He was so fast that he would then trap my arms. As he was demonstrating, he shut his eyes. The art was so flowing and it was obvious why he was the teacher of the teachers. He was outstanding.

Sifu Kwok teaching me Wing Chun basics

To further my healing, I was blessed with Sifu Kwok finishing the evening performing acupressure on me. My back was such a mess that it took him so much longer to work out the scar tissue and knots. As I said,

"It hurt so good!" In a point where my Qi flow was blocked, it hurt when he pushed on the point. Then, the pain would go away. Having learned a little bit in my massage training, I knew what to expect and that I would feel better afterwards.

That evening and the next day my back felt wonderful. Sitting all day is so hard on my back. I am sure that some of the pain that I have down my legs is from the pressure in my back. What a difference his working my back made. Even luckier, when I saw Sifu at an event the next day, he started doing acupressure on my legs. He had me stand to see if I could lock out my knees, which I normally was challenged to do. Holding on to Steve, I stood up and locked my knee for seconds. This was definitely an improvement. Steve was shown the major points so that we could continue to work my legs, especially since the next day I had a new point on my knee that had some sensation. Immediate improvement was unexpected, but Dr. Kwok being named "Miracle Man is very appropriate."

"A goal is not always meant to be reached; it often serves simply as something to aim at.

~ Bruce Lee

Looking at all I have had to deal with in my life since the crash, I realize that I often exclaim, "I CAN STILL DO IT!" I am grateful for the resilience of the human spirit which my life has exemplified, for the wonderful support I have received from my family and friends, and for my faith that has carried me through it all. My hope now is that my story can inspire and motivate other people to push through their personal obstacles and achieve their goals and exclaim, "I can do it!"

Chapter 10
Moving from Yesterday to Today

Keeping the memories, yet moving into the present was challenging. I had to find a way to make new happy memories.

One of the hardest things to do was to live in the moment, especially when I had more capabilities before the accident. My mind constantly went back to what I could do before or what I had accomplished. Living in the present and only thinking about today was difficult for me. A truth that I once was told was: "It doesn't matter what you did in the past; it only matters what you are doing today." This thought made me realize that it didn't really matter what all my accomplishments were; it only mattered what good I was doing today. It hit home as my life had changed so dramatically.

I knew that I had a choice of living in the yesteryears or moving into today. It was important to think about what I could do and not what I was giving up. No wonder so many people with life-changing events deal with depression; how do you stay away from going dark? It was easy to remember all the great things that I used to do, but I had to make a choice and learn to figure out all the things that I could do now.

As easy as it may sound, this thinking is a process. For me, I looked back at what I could do before and organized them into three categories: what I could easily do now, the ones that I would have to learn a new way to do, and the activities I would just have to avoid. To start with, my body was and a mess and I was healing, so just getting through the day was challenging. Eventually, I became stronger and found ways to do the everyday tasks without walking. I added in many of my sports, adaptively. The biggest challenge was giving up what I just couldn't do. At least if I wanted to, my walking was replaced with rolling, running could be replaced with racing in a wheelchair, hiking with horseback riding, and surfing with lying on a board. I had no excuse. I could get back out there!

Because I never did well with being told that "I can't" do something, not being able to scuba dive didn't go over well. In the hospital, I was so excited to meet a paraplegic that scuba dove. He even invited me to dive with him, and so I had planned to meet him the summer after the accident. Strangely lucky after I had been rehabbing and at an appointment, I was excitedly telling my general doctor that I was going diving in Monterey. She looked at me and sternly said, "You punctured your lung and can't dive. It will explode if you dive." I was crushed!

Not taking "no" for an answer, I met with a wonderful lung doctor. After all the tests, my results weren't acceptable. Dr. Mar said that I couldn't scuba dive but I could snorkel. I explained, "I love scuba diving, I really don't like snorkeling because it is just not as fun for me. Is there any way that I can dive?" After a long discussion, he agreed that I could go to twenty feet, but no deeper. He saw my contorted face and continued by saying, "You can dive deeper, below an atmosphere, as long as you have a doctor dive with you who could re-inflate your lung when it bursts upon surfacing." With that visual, I got the point, although my mind kept jumping back to one of my favorite trips.

Snorkeling in the Caribbean

Before the crash and the third time we travelled to Belize, the trip consisted of a dive trip combined with instructing cave rescue training. Our first two times to Belize were student rescue training, again starting with scuba diving. Knowing that there was a high possibility for injury during the cave rescue training, we always began the trip by going scuba diving in the Caribbean. This time, at off-season, we had our own private island right on Belize's Great Barrier Reef. At this rustic resort, fresh meals were made for us and we had a dive master that took us out on all types of dives. The room was just what I had imagined—our own cabin right at the waters' edge. The "but" came in when this cabin along the beach with the lulling waves turned into a nightmare. The open windows (no glass) allowed wind and the storming rain to come in. First the bounding thunder and lightning flashes woke us up, and then the wet raindrops blew through the windows onto the bed and our faces every night when it stormed. We were sleep deprived, but what a wonderful experience anyway. And, we experienced the most amazing dives in the world plus the food made up for the lack of sleep.

Each morning, after using the tiny bathroom with a dirt floor, we would make a dive before our breakfast, which included homemade waffles and fresh seafood. One of our dives went like this: Steve and I rolled off the dive boat into the clear Caribbean water and started our decent. At first we stopped at about 20 feet to get our bearings and looked at the moving vegetation in the coral wall and fish that were very brightly colored passing us by. As we dove the colors muted, but we still saw very interesting sea life. My favorite was a small school of sea horses that I swam by. They were so cute! There was so much to see in this sea garden. I poked my face towards a hole and right at my mask came lobster claws, startling me. I immediately moved backwards (probably jumped). Luckily it was easy in the water to see. The lobster was huge, or so it seemed. We continued enjoying the beautiful sea life, going down to over 100 feet and then back to 30 feet until our tanks hit 800 PSI or our dive computers signaled us to head for the surface.

Three dives each day was heaven, especially when we had a night dive (after sunset). The clear bright blue water was black at night except within the flashlight rays. Good thing that I wasn't claustrophobic; the small area that I could see made me feel like I was in a box. It was so worth it because many different critters came out at night. The electric eel was a bit spooky to see with its very large teeth, and the poisonous stone fish was very hard to notice camouflaged in the sand, where we were careful not to brush against it.

Every time we came back in from diving, the freshly caught fish would be waiting for us. Since I loved fresh food and was always hungry after a good work out, I was thrilled. They treated us so well that we felt like royalty. The time on our own island went by too fast.

After having this amazing start to our vacation, on our own island, diving one of the most beautiful reefs in the world, we went inland to help teach local guides a rope rescue course. As my memories go back to the diving and then the inland training, I realized that as a paraplegic, it would be extremely difficult to even remotely repeat diving and the cave rescue. I could, in fact, snorkel and see brightly colored fish and vegetation. However, to mimic the cave rescue training would be very tough although our instructor, Bruce Hagan, is up for the challenge.

Traveling to the inland jungle of Belize was the contrast to the Cayes. Every day was different, hiking through the jungle, trekking through a cave, or rappelling and hauling litter teams up sink holes after building rope systems. The fourteen students and six instructors spent a week training in all these skills to be ready for a final scenario.

Finally, we were at the last day, preparing for the final scenario. The locating and rescuing of the injured patient in the waterfall cave was driven by the students, and us instructors were just support insuring the scenario went safely. As the rescue scenario progressed through the long cave using rope systems to safely move the patient, the water in the cave started rising from a torrential rainstorm up on the surface that we were unaware of. It rose to a point that we knew that the eighteen-inch-high entrance to the cave was now underwater and we were trapped in this waterfall cave. We wouldn't be able to crawl through with the rising water; it was impassable. It was raining so hard on the surface that the water was rushing down the subterranean river and even dripping through the cave ceiling that was previously dry.

Our only alternative was to get to high-ground and wait until the water level dropped. With one instructor, the students hiked back to the "safe" high-ground area where they sat and waited, enjoying their own backpack treats as well as goodies left in my backpack sitting on a rock from our logistics plan. The five of us instructors plus two students remained in the back, picking up all the equipment. We took down all the rope systems, disconnecting anchors, hardware, and freeing the ropes.

The water continued to rise so we decided to make it to high-ground and wait until the water subsided. We didn't know how long we would be there, an hour or days. At least we had four backpacks. Between the packs we had enough supplies for survival for several days. We had a great time, eating what we had in Steve's pack, using Steve's water purification tablets, drinking what was in another pack, and telling crazy stories of training and rescues.

Eventually, maybe three hours later, two of the Belizean guides showed up. We were very surprised until the lead guide explained that we had been gone more than eighteen hours and it had been pouring rain, so he thought that he should come check on us. The rain had stopped and we still weren't back. With his years of experience, he thought that we might be stuck. At the cave entrance, the guide waited until he saw the water level drop enough, and then he crawled through the eighteen- inch-high entrance/exit and got to us. Once he reached us, we knew that we didn't have much time to get through as the rains from the mountains would soon reach us and flood the entrance again. As instructors, we moved our team out through the high ground picking up the group of students. We quickly (probably an hour) made it to the exit after passing through the most beautiful white stalactite formations. It was special ground to the Mayans, and we knew why after that experience. We got everyone out of the cave and into the jungle. We then had to figure out how to cross the river that had swollen to three times its size and speed from the rain, but at least we were out of the cave. We eventually made it back to camp safely. Thankfully we went when we did or we would have been trapped in the cave for a few days.

Of course, today, life for us is really different. The only way that I could have even gone through the jungle or the cave would be in a stretcher. And for the real-life rescue, I would have been in big trouble. We would have figured it out, but the ease of movement isn't there; and it would have taken four people to carry me in the stretcher. To consider doing such an adventure, I would have to be patient, rely on others, and set-up equipment to make it work.

Activities and travel are just done adaptively. I have to forget the "I can't" and know that "*I CAN STILL DO IT!*" Otherwise, it could wear me down not being able to do things or travel the same way combining training, adventure, hiking, climbing, and diving. I focus on creating activities and fun trips that I can do. It is surprising how much I really can do. Since our idea of relaxation is constantly doing something, we just have to figure out what would work to keep busy. As I remembered the Belizean trip, I ask myself, "How can I turn this trip into the same exhilaration now that I am in a wheelchair?"

Ready to take off from Williamsburg, Virginia

Another great bank of memories is private plane flying. As the pilot, we took short trips to visit TJ at school; and Steve, Lindsay, and I did a west coast to east coast trip and back among other trips. I always felt closer to heaven up in the air and so loved flying. An example of one of our trips was when we were celebrating TJ's 21st birthday and picking up a horse from a friend. I flew TJ, his friend, and Lindsay from San Jose through the desert, past military bases to Las Vegas. Staying on The Strip, we celebrated for two days. I left the boys to continue the celebration until I returned. In the meantime, Lindsay and I flew directly to my friend Sue Henderson's home in Arizona. Sue had offered to give me her sweetheart of a horse, Josie, since she was too short for her daughter and her. We were especially lucky to be the recipients since I had planned to take English Riding lessons in my retirement and Lindsay wanted to improve her western riding.

To get Josie home, Lindsay and I met Steve at Sue's home. He had driven all the way from our home in his truck with a friend's empty horse trailer. He was glad to be at Sue's after the 12-hour drive and relax with good friends. We enjoyed thought-provoking discussions and Sue spoiled us with an amazing country dinner.

The next morning before we were to leave, we all took turns riding this awesome horse. Josie, a beautiful Bay Quarter Horse, responded well to each one of us riding her. We said goodbye to our friends as I flew alone back to Las Vegas and Steve and Lindsay loaded Josie in the trailer. Pulling a horse trailer would take time for them to get back, since it was a long haul for Josie. While Steve drove, I flew into Vegas and the boys picked me up at the closest small airport to The Strip. Since I was staying the night, I got to have fun and celebrate with the boys. This time all three of us were over 21 and able to really celebrate just before the boys went back to college.

Thinking about the great part of this memory, I know I could repeat most of the events and do them adaptively. Although I haven't flown since the crash, I would love to. I would have to learn to fly a plane that is all hand controls, but it is something that is available. I am sure that it would be just like my old days of flying and similar to driving a car using hand controls as I do now.

Traveling in Vegas is easy, since I can roll around everywhere. The challenge would come in visiting people with homes that have steps into the house, small doorways, or two stories. The solution would be to just stay in a hotel with an adaptive room. If I hadn't flown, I could have driven in our motor home (with adaptive hand controls). Since I brought my room with me, I could just stay in the motor home.

There are memories that I have decided to just keep as memories. Every weekend in Hawaii, there was a race and/or a parade. Whether it was just a running race up Diamond Head or a triathlon out of Ala Moana, we participated every weekend. To stay in shape, during the week we would run in the morning, swim at lunch, and bicycle at night. We had so much fun staying in shape, in order to not feel guilty when we finished each race with the reward of Malasadas (fried Portuguese sweet bread). We even continued racing in triathlons when we moved back to California from Hawaii.

New challenging memories keep replacing old memories. All of these adventures include my husband. I could travel or go on adventures by myself, like flying to a meeting in Los Angeles and returning the same day, which I have done twice. But, it is much easier to go with my wonderful husband. I am so lucky because we have a rhythm and make it look easy. We continue to figure out how to make every adventure work, especially since we don't sit still.

"You can do whatever you put your mind to."
~ Ben Franklin

This quote mimics one of my favorite Bible verses:

"If you believe, whatever you ask for in prayer, you will receive."
~ Matthew 21:22

And, I really believe that as a paraplegic—or anyone for that matter—we can do more than we ever thought we could. In early martial arts, I learned that the body could do so much more than the mind typically allows. Just try it. Everything that seems a limitation, I push through it and be creative to see what I can do.

Although my life is considered different, I have always pushed it or gone beyond the expectations, even in pain, in order to continue making great memories.

Chapter 11
Living with Pain

Handling chronic pain is perhaps the biggest
long-term challenge for me as a paraplegic.

Riding around Lake Calero

As an EMT, I have learned that each person's pain tolerance is
different. Though I have a high tolerance for pain, it is of little comfort,

except when I think of others who might perceive more pain because of their low tolerance. I try not to complain because there is nothing others can do about it. In my case, the pain comes from the compromised nerves in my lower back telling my brain that my legs hurt.

What many able-bodied people don't understand is the pain that we paraplegics are in most of the time. While everyone's pain threshold is different, chronic pain is debilitating. When I was first injured, the doctors said about 50 percent of paraplegics felt pain from their injury. Much later, I learned that it is close to 80 percent of those with spinal-cord traumas have pain. Personally, I just live with mine, but it is more often present than not, like a background noise or louder.

Medical professionals often ask their patients what level of pain they are experiencing on a scale between 1 and 10—10 being the worst. Since I am curious and have tracked my pain for a medical study, I have learned that my pain level averages out at about 4 on a daily basis. Strangely, if I needed to ride in an ambulance today and give the paramedics that number or higher, they would probably give me an IV with pain medication. When my pain reaches 8, it is close to unbearable, similar to childbirth or a major bone dislocation. That's a lot to cope with, so I try to find ways to lessen the pain. One way is to take nerve-pain blockers, which I do three times a day. If I go past the time to take the medicine, my pain level can spike. I clock when to take the pills because it takes about a half hour for them to kick in. Also, I don't want to take addictive pain medications, so I try to manage with the neurological ones.

> **"The secret of success is learning**
> **how to use pain and pleasure**
> **instead of having pain and pleasure use you.**
> **If you do that, you're in control."**
> ~ Tony Robbins

The two factors that influence my pain level the most are sitting and exercise. If I sit all day, especially long days, my legs really hurt. It feels as though saran wrap is tightly wrapped around each leg, pinching it. Another sensation is the heaviness in my legs, as though they were made of cement. Every once in a while, I get the worst pain, which feels like a burning sensation. When I get this pain, as much as I try, I can't ignore it in order to focus on other activities.

Exercise can be an amazing relief for me. While I am exercising, the pain decreases or goes away. And after the exercise, I may be pain-free or in a low level of pain for a couple of hours. The pain I can get from exercise "hurts so good," of course, because it's from working muscles. It's productive and positive. I find that horseback riding is the very best exercise for my chronic pain. It works many of the muscles in my legs, core, neck, and arms; and I have the added benefit of being outdoors. Gaiting and cantering are the most fun: the vibration of the horse's movement helps relieve the pain.

Biking on my FES cycle and walking in parallel bars are also helpful for decreasing the pain and getting my heart rate up. Water skiing and snow skiing are useful because they require that I work my legs, even though I am strapped in. Any activity that gets me outside in the beauty of nature and requires a focus on technique helps cardio strength as well as decreasing the focus on pain. Distraction is a powerful force in alleviating pain! Even the cold is useful, since I seem to do better in it than in heat.

Swimming is also a short-term cure. I don't notice the pain when I am floating or swimming in a pool or a lake, although, within an hour afterward, it comes back in full force. Hot tubs only work for me when I am in them. As soon as I get out, the pain actually increases for a while.

"Pain is inevitable; suffering is optional."
~ M. Kathleen Casey

When I am home and can lie down, I have found that lying on my side in the fetal position usually drops my pain level, especially after a long day at work. Most of the time, twenty to thirty minutes of lying down can help. Nighttime sleep is a great relief, too. Every once in a great while, pain wakes me up in the middle of the night, and then it's hard to get back to sleep because my mind starts working on all that I need to do. I wasn't very functional without eight hours of sleep before the crash, and I'm even less functional now, since the level of pain seems to rise if I am sleep-deprived.

Flying also increases my pain, whether I am lying down or sitting. It seems that the barometric pressure is a factor. Sometimes when I fly, I have to take a higher dose of my neurological medicine or a dose of the mild (addictive) pain meds that I rarely take otherwise. Besides my legs, I get pain in my lower back or left side at the hip-hugger waistband level. I have found that by applying Lidocaine, Arnicare gel, or Pain-a-Trate locally, I can sometimes calm the level of pain there and down my legs. Another way I can reduce my pain is by using the acupressure that I learned from a martial-arts massage class. I also treat myself to a massage now and then, and I typically get weekly treatments of scalp acupuncture, for they can lessen the pain.

I've learned that talking about my pain doesn't help, so I try to "just grin and bear it." That's why this chapter is shorter than the others! But I recognize and empathize with others that pain is debilitating and can be depressing. My psychological antidote is to exercise, to focus on other good things, or to think about how much I can do versus how much worse my situation could be. We might not have survived the crash, for instance, or my passengers could have been injured more severely. I might have had a lasting head injury or more severe permanent injuries. With this perspective and my religious faith, I have been able to cope with the chronic pain and enjoy my life.

Like so many crises and challenges in life, I've found it's best to focus on the gift of life and to deal with the struggle. My mantra is to "be positive and push through it," not to belabor it. So far, it's working for me, and I am doing more in my life than I initially thought I could as a paraplegic.

Chapter 12
The Fun of Travel—
Seeing the World

Since it can be challenging to fly as a paraplegic,
travel now includes the benefits
of cruise ships and motor homes.

I've had a love of travel all of my life. At a young age, my parents took my brother and me camping almost every weekend during the spring and summer months. The summer before I graduated from college, my best friend, Holly Vargas, and I traveled throughout Europe on a First Class Eurail Pass, staying at youth hostels. We had so much fun, meeting the local people and going on many adventures. I preferred seeing history rather than reading about it in school! Later, I went on a short trip to Hawaii with Holly during my early professional work life. It was on this trip that I met the love of my life, my husband, Steve. He had gotten dragged to the Officers Club at Hickam Air Force Base and my aunt and uncle were stationed there. They had taken Holly and me to the club to celebrate Holly continuing on to Australia. My heart jumped when I walked in and saw this handsome man sitting across the room. Yes, it was love at first sight, which I previously didn't believe in. We danced all night and then stayed up all the next night talking at his company luau. It was like we had been long-time friends with all the commonalities. He and I were both into athletics—he was in the Army and I was a business woman—and we both shared a love of seeing new places, while enjoying our outdoor sports and physical challenges. We continued on the same path once we got married and I moved to Hawaii; we had both worked hard so we could play hard! We loved traveling all over the world, melding into the culture, and even learning a little of the languages.

When we weren't sightseeing or eating the local fare, we were running, hiking, scuba diving, or horseback riding, to name a few of the activities.

Even with our small children, we traveled to foreign countries. Traveling in Asia with blonde children proved to be interesting, but our ability to speak Japanese and the love of the countries helped offset the novelty. And, we stayed active by walking or hiking everywhere with the kids in backpacks and holding our hands.

After the crash, I really wanted to resume the life we had before, so I was determined to discover ways that would help me navigate traveling nationally and internationally. Being with Steve was important to my success in reaching this goal, because he literally carried me up steps or lifted me into vehicles when needed.

Even traveling from Silicon Valley to Tahoe Vista and then to Northstar to ski and continue our ski-patrol activities involved a lot more planning and managing logistics. After the four-hour drive from Los Gatos, just figuring out my clothing, food, and bathroom breaks was challenging. Dealing with the extreme cold and the sporadic pain I was in from sitting in my wheelchair so much added to the complexity.

As great as having our family place on the beautiful lake in Tahoe was, it wasn't enough traveling for me, though. About six months after I was home from the hospital and a number of trips to Tahoe, we found a used motor home (RV) with a factory installed wheelchair lift and other accommodations for a wheelchair user. The bed was almost the right height to transfer into, and I had a roll-in shower, for instance. Though I didn't appreciate RVs before the crash, because I had planned to fly and stay in hotels, I now saw them as my chance to travel more easily. I could lie down in the back, on the soft couch, or in the plush coach seat while Steve was driving. Our first outing was to the coast while I was still coaching girls' soccer. The RV worked amazingly well, and it was so much better than the campers that I had grown up with. And, the best part of this RV was that I could reach most everything in it except the high cabinets. We had a number of soccer tournaments in Northern California, and we brought the RV so that the girls could hang out. The whole team could fit inside between games. We would bring in lunch and the girls would devour the sandwiches while they relaxed with the air conditioning on.

Depending where we travelled to, Steve had to do a lot of carrying— our luggage, groceries, occasionally me, etc.—sometimes up and down stairs, especially at our cabin at Lake Tahoe. Although my dad built a ramp to the cabin right away, the kitchen and family room were upstairs. The only time I ventured to the second floor was when someone, usually Steve, carried me. There were days that I just stayed down in our bedroom so that he didn't have to carry me. Luckily, my father and brother eventually installed an elevator for me.

Even with the RV, it was great when we stayed in a location with a pool. Some pools had lifts to get me in or I would have to drop in. Once in the water, I swam laps or stood at the edge holding on to the bar with Steve stabilizing my knees. The biggest challenge was getting me out of the water. I would use the lift if there was one and it worked or Steve would have to carry me out.

Our RV has a lift which makes it easy to get me in

The beauty of the RV was that as we travelled we could stop wherever and whenever we wanted to. For most of the better locations, we did need a reservation. We went to Disneyland in Anaheim, California. At Disneyland, Steve would pick me up from the wheelchair and transfer me onto a ride if I couldn't transfer myself. I was able to go on every ride that I wanted to. It was so much fun! Some of the rides were jerky, and it must have been funny to watch me moving a lot. I would try to stabilize myself using my core instead of my legs.

Later we took a family trip to Yellowstone, Wyoming, via Utah to visit my brother. Whenever there was pavement, short grass, or hard dirt, I could roll to our destination within the parks. I even got to see the geysers, being careful to not get too close. We stopped by the best milkshake stand in Jackson Hole for a deliciously smooth yet crunchy huckleberry milkshake. And, we could make a quick stop by the river running parallel to the road so TJ could catch us a good trout for breakfast.

We used the RV to take the kids and their friends places also. The kids had fun, sleeping in the comfortable sofa bed. Later, we took the RV to go camping and horseback riding. After a ride or two on beautiful trails, we would entertain out of it. The RV had an oven, so we could bake to make an even more delectable dinner with desert. We had fun travelling all around the United States.

Having been on cruises several times as an able-bodied person, I knew that we could travel more easily on a cruise. My first real travel out of the country was a cruise—to Mexico. We took our RV to Long Beach and boarded the ship there. The cruise line had an ADA bedroom for me, and I could go most places on the ship.

Like any previous cruise trip, I wanted to take advantage of each port and go on excursions. When the ship's excursion staff wouldn't let me kayak in Cabo San Lucas, we opted to swim with the dolphins. It didn't take much effort on my part for them to pull me along in the water. Swimming in the warm ocean was fun, too. Sightseeing in historic Puerto Vallarta reminded me how beautiful the town was and made it my favorite port.

Swimming with a dolphin in Cabo San Lucas, Mexico

While my preference was flying before, it was so much easier for me to travel by RV or ship. Steve didn't have to keep transferring luggage, and a bed was always handy. As I've mentioned, if I had to sit for a long time, I usually experienced less pain if I could lie down for a while.

I learned that one of the best physical therapies I could do when traveling was swimming. The other workout that I tried to do every day was standing using my braces with a walker or "standing" in a pool with Steve guarding my knees to ensure that they did not buckle.

Our next trip was to Alaska, and our RV allowed us to visit friends along the way to Seattle where we boarded. Once we are on a ship, it is always essential for me to have an ADA-appropriate room; but on this trip, we didn't have one even though we had reserved one. Luckily, a kind passenger switched rooms with us.

Two of the highlights of this trip were traveling across a glacier near Seward in a dog sled and sea kayaking near Ketchikan. For my first time kayaking since the accident, I didn't mind sliding down in the seat with each stroke; I was out in the ocean!

Dog sledding on a glacier in Alaska

Although I loved flying, it really didn't love me, whether on trips to Panama for stem-cell treatments, trips to Boston for a pain-management trial, or flying to London for a cruise. I would be in pain for the duration of the flight, despite being in the bulkhead near the front of the plane. The other challenge was using the bathrooms. Steve either had to carry me to the toilet or lift me there from the awkward aisle chair, squeezing us through the narrow bathroom door.

For our niece's wedding, we combined the trip with a week-long physical therapy training in Baltimore. The equipment was sophisticated, and I used a machine that stimulated my muscles so that I could walk. What amazed us was how much better the rehab for paraplegics was Back East, although the East was not as up-to-date on ADA accommodations as California was. When we would go out for dinner, we often had to enter the restaurant through the kitchen and seldom found an adaptive bathroom for wheelchair users.

Another time, we snuck away to Maui with Lindsay and a friend of hers. Again, the flight was tough, but the timeshare was workable. I was in heaven: I was able to body surf right off the beach. I loved it because I forgot that I wasn't kicking to ride the wave. When we went to another beach to snorkel, Steve carried me into the water. Once we were deep enough that I could swim, I pulled the mask onto my face and headed out to the breakwater, swimming at a smooth pace. We had to swim about 200 yards before we could see any marine life. After snorkeling until we were waterlogged, we headed back, and—much to my delight—a lifeguard rushed toward us with a beach wheelchair! It had big, fat tires, and he rolled it right into the water for me to climb into. How I wish these special beach chairs weren't so expensive!

I found that I had to be alert and creative as a paraplegic. Once, on a trip to Louisville, Kentucky, for a funeral, Steve and I were swimming in the hotel pool, which thankfully had a lift. As the lift lowered to my chair's height, I transferred into the wheelchair soaking wet. And, I noticed that it seemed lopsided. After looking at the components of the chair, I discovered that it had a flat tire. Although we had always traveled with an extra tube, we had gone four years without a flat! I had to go back into the pool while Steve changed the tube and then I got back into the wheelchair.

Sight-seeing in San Juan, Puerto Rico

Several years after the crash, we decided to fly to Florida with the family and go on a Caribbean cruise. We visited the Pirates of the Caribbean at Disneyworld before cruising into the Eastern Caribbean from Miami. What a trip: We enjoyed Puerto Rico's charm and St. Maarten's shops. In St. Thomas, we went snorkeling with turtles and I discovered the sea-scooter, an underwater motorized propulsion vehicle that pulled me through the water. If I wiggled rather than paddled, I could stay flat. Although I couldn't look up as well as I would have liked because of my neck fusion, I could snorkel and be out in the ocean—one of my favorite places to be.

Rolling down the streets of Stockholm, Sweden

Steve and I traveled to a number of states either by RV or plane for business, fun, or my treatments. We covered a portion of the Midwest, the Southwest, and the West. When we were in Mississippi taking my water ski lessons with Bill, we had the added bonus of learning more about the South by going to the exciting city of New Orleans.

After traveling in the United States and overseas, we had gained a lot of experience about what worked and didn't for us while traveling. We had always wanted to go to Northern Europe, so we decided to brave it. We chose a two-week cruise to Belgium, Germany, Estonia, Russia, Finland, Sweden, and Denmark. Every country was beautiful, and we had the most fun meeting Scott Yoder, a college friend in Finland. The history in Germany was especially interesting to me, since it is the country of my ancestry.

What I learned from all of these travels, above all, was to have patience and good planning. I had to make sure that I had everything I needed for comfort, unanticipated problems, and any delays. In order to get my plane seat set up, I had to board first and then get off last. It made for a much longer flight time, just sitting in the plane. No wonder I had a high pain level most of the time. On the way to the plane, I had to go through security and wait for an available female to pat me down. Sometimes that delayed my boarding process too. One time, I faced an inquisition because I had rolled through my garden, which had ammonium nitrate from fertilizer in the soil. Not a good chemical to have on your wheels at the airport!

So, there were constant surprises and "learning experiences." It helped to build up a tolerance for both rudeness and kindness. Several times, the airlines lost my luggage. This is very disconcerting, since, as a paraplegic, the carry-on bags can't carry everything you need. At least they found the bags a day later. Another time, when I was rolling over the lip in the ramp to enter an airplane, the little wheels of my chair caught, and I was thrown forward onto the aisle of the aircraft. While most people were kind and considerate, some were not. If you can believe it, a couple of people on that flight walked right over my body as I struggled to get back into the chair. I guess they were impatient to get to their seats.

Family trip to Universal Studios watching movie set explosions

Travels all over the world

I have often thought that my motto should be, "Have wheels, will travel." Innovations are being developed every day to help paraplegics enjoy as full a life as possible. For this I am grateful.

Chapter 13
Keeping the Faith

My faith has made a difference in my life, sustaining me through the tough times.

If faith is defined as belief in something larger than oneself, I feel fortunate that I was raised in a Christian home, because my faith has

sustained me through-out my life. When I fell in love with Steve, one of the huge draws was that he was also a Christian, and we shared three bonds: spiritual, physical, and mental. If I didn't have such a strong faith, dealing with the accident and all of the life changes that came afterwards would have been even tougher for me.

Still in love after all these years

It is ironic that growing up, I always thought that kids that had gone through some type of trauma or tribulation were better Christians. I would listen to their testimonies at our summer camps at Hume Lake, and I felt like kids that had a simple past like me took their faith for granted. I learned from these friends with the challenges but didn't fully get it. Now I understand their passion in their faith, and for me almost dying put my faith and life into perspective. The experience showed me what was really important in life: God first, then family, and then everything else. These lessons of life helped me realize that every one of us deals with troubles or pain. There were days when I wondered, in fact, how someone would get through it all without faith. Every once in a while, the nerve pain would be so great that it brought tears to my eyes. But, because of my faith, I could look past the pain.

"The future is as bright as your faith."
~ Thomas S. Monson

Various doctors told me that I would never walk again. It was so discouraging to me, because doctors really shouldn't take away hope. My immediate thought when I heard that comment was, "You aren't God, so you don't know for sure." I know it was my belief in God and my internal will to fight that gave me the courage to keep pushing my body to improve and my mind to stay positive. Everyone needs hope, even if just a little. One day I asked one of the doctors that treated me why anyone would tell someone with an injury like mine that he/she would never walk again. He gave me a simple (but unacceptable to me) answer: "Doctors have to state the facts." I reasoned, "How could anyone rule out what might be possible?" We still don't know everything about how our brain, spinal column, and nervous system work and work together. There might be progress in our knowledge through science. I also wanted my muscles and body to be strong simply for the health benefits. So, I kept pushing myself. And, whether or not I could walk again on earth, I believe that I will walk again in heaven. This belief also encouraged me.

Another benefit of my faith was my belief that God put things in my life for me to learn from, and to prepare me for the challenges ahead. My schooling gave me the knowledge of how my body was injured and how it might heal. For instance, I had been in advanced placement classes in the sciences in high school. In college, I minored in biology and chemistry and had an upper-division class in anatomy and physiology. All of this knowledge served me well while undergoing all of the medical procedures I had to endure after the crash. I already knew so much about the body and how little we know compared to what there is yet to learn, especially about the body's control centers.

When I was in college, for example, it was common knowledge that nerves could not regenerate when damaged. The "fact" that science has now determined that nerves can regenerate gives me hope. My Emergency Medical Training (EMT) furthered my comprehension of how my body reacted internally to the trauma and what I could expect from the healing. I also understood the best ways to expedite some of the healing: what areas I could push in rehab and which areas needed to rest.

The most challenging was knowing why I was having pain and that I would need some drugs to alleviate it or at least calm it.

How other people have dealt with the challenges in their lives also taught me a lot. One very special person was a Realtor™ I recruited to join the real estate firm I was with. I actually grew to think of her as an angel sent from God. She introduced me to her husband, who had ALS (Lou Gehrig's disease). I could see more life and spirit in his eyes than I saw in many able-bodied people. This couple showed me the importance of making the best of whatever life has given you. Charlie and Lucy Wedemeyer lived their lives, despite his condition—going on speaking tours and keeping their own faith alive while inspiring others. He passed away not long after I got out of the hospital, and I felt fortunate to have known him.

Another way that I was prepared for my own traumatic event was when I was called upon to perform first aid on the slopes during my ski patrol work. A skier had broken his neck and was paralyzed. Although I had learned a lot about spinal trauma through my studies, I had never had to deal with it in actuality. As tough as the situation was, I believe God put this situation in my path to help me deal with my own trauma, yet to come. The experience taught me so much about what to expect. When I had the accident and started my recovery process, I had a better visual about what was happening in my body.

I know our family's Christian faith helped our daughter through her challenges as a result of the crash, too. Our prayers were answered when she healed from her spinal fusion and was able to go back to school soon after her recovery.

To this day, I believe that God will never give you more than you can handle. Since I have had so many tough situations in my life, I joke to my family, "I guess God must think highly of me to keep putting these challenges in my life." As a result of surviving the crash and then getting spinal meningitis, I felt that I have a purpose to fulfill—and God still wants me on earth. I am still waiting for that purpose to be revealed to me. Perhaps writing this book is one way for me to help others.

I haven't spoken too much about depression in this book, but most medical professionals expect that people with paralysis will get depressed, if not suicidal. The doctors kept trying to give me anti-depression meds. I refused because I didn't think I needed them, and I didn't believe suicide was an option (because of my faith). I understood, however, how a person could feel suicidal if he or she had a sense of hopelessness. Sometimes, too, the body's chemical changes from an accident or depression can throw one into a potentially suicidal state. Luckily, I didn't go there.

I get how hard it is to push through pain and major trauma, and I can't imagine how hard it would be without having a strong faith! Every day, prayers kept me focused on what was important in my recovery and kept my faith strong. I believed in this statement from Matthew 21:22: "If you believe, you will receive whatever you ask for in prayer." Having such a strong faith and reminding myself of biblical verses really made a difference in my recovery. My favorite verse that really applied to my new life challenges was found in Proverbs 3:5: "Trust in the Lord with all your heart and do not depend on your own understanding." Another encouraging verse that would pop into my mind sometimes was Psalms 31:24: "Be strong and take heart, all you who hope in the Lord." These verses helped me through my days. To start my day right, I would try to read a verse every morning when I woke up. A verse like Ephesians 6:10: "Be strong in the Lord and in his mighty power" helped me overcome the pain I sometimes felt upon awakening in the morning.

I am grateful for the faith that I share with my family. It has made all the difference in my life with this new challenge of paraplegia. And it has been vital to my recovery and my attitude. I really don't know how well I would have done without my Christian beliefs.

Chapter 14
Giving Back

*Grateful for survival. I am dedicated now
to helping others learn how
to approach life's adversities and challenges.*

From a young age, I have always thrived on helping others. I might have partially developed this desire to "give back" from all the fortunate experiences I enjoyed as a child. I was born to parents who worked very hard and cared deeply about their family and friends. Working hard and being extremely frugal afforded them the opportunity to move to a very small ranch in Northern California when I started high school. My brother and I had happy childhoods, even though they were filled with many responsibilities. Even as a preteen and teen, I enjoyed babysitting children while helping them with their schoolwork. It was so gratifying to watch them learn and grow. I also found that the best way to learn something thoroughly was to teach it.

I must have inherited a streak of curiosity as well. I always wondered how things worked and how to fix them, when needed. This trait would especially come in handy after I became paralyzed. It was also important to me as a mom and a happily married woman. With our own lifestyle of hard work, we vacationed together as avidly as we lived the other parts of our lives. Because of our approach to living balanced lives, I was highly motivated to continue positioning God, family, work, and sports—in that order—after the crash.

As I moved from adolescence to adulthood, volunteering my time and knowledge became even more important to me. In college, I was the rush chairman (recruiter) for my sorority, Alpha Phi. Later, out of school, I gave back to my sorority sisters by overseeing their house as the sorority corporation's board president. Having kids, it was easy to be involved with their sports activities. Being on the local board for the Pop Warner and Cheer organization and the business manager for several football teams, it was rewarding to help create great programs and opportunities for the players and cheerleaders. During my years of coaching my kids' recreational and competitive soccer teams under the Los Gatos United Soccer League, I loved being able to help the team members improve by passing along the experience from my own athletic pursuits and the expertise I received from athletic professionals.

When I saw the players on the soccer team use a new way to pass the ball to a teammate that I had shown them or benefit from a life lesson from something we discussed, it was rewarding. The common vision we as coaches developed and instilled in the teammates helped these players achieve more and play better than they could individually. On a breakaway to goal, for instance, the team was more likely to score a point when the player with the ball passed to a teammate instead of trying to make the shot himself.

Likewise, as a rescue instructor teaching a rescuer how to get off a rope while caught in a rope system, how to build a haul system, or even teaching first aid to business men and women was equally satisfying. The ultimate reward was when a rope accident was prevented or when someone used his or her first-aid skills to save a life.

Giving back for me is often manifested in coaching or instructing. For years before the accident, I taught children and adults martial arts. Whether it was how to throw a kick or protect yourself using a self-defense technique, I felt like I was making a difference teaching. When I was able to get back to training in martial arts, I was pleasantly surprised and thrilled when I could teach safety and self-defense. Later, I even helped teach many other techniques in my martial art classes.

Because I interface with so many different people through my various pursuits, I see what an effect attitude has on one's ability to be successful, even when facing adversity. I am grateful for the "can do" attitude that I have. I have always told my students and players: "Just try." My rationale is, if you don't try, you won't know if you can do it. It's worth a try. The results can be surprising. I believe that part of the "can do" attitude is not only doing your best but also giving back to others.

When the crash happened, suddenly this love of helping others—one of my personal motivators and pleasures—came to a screeching halt. I could do little myself, let alone help anyone else. In the first hospital, I was so braced up and in such pain that my family and the nurses had to do most things for me. Even later, at VMC, I needed a lot of help, and it was hard for me to ask for it. It wasn't an issue of pride or ego; it was a role reversal for me. It was foreign to me to have to ask someone to provide me with help. I evidentially learned and was astonished at how willing most people were to be of help. For example, later I had to ask perfect strangers to pull my wheelchair out of the back of my car (if I hadn't disassembled it) or carry my cup of coffee (if I had forgotten a thermos) back to my office. Focusing on the kindnesses of others energized my positive attitude, instead of frustrating me that I couldn't do something for myself in that moment. I was so thankful.

As I have explained earlier, after my accident, I expected to be asked to step down from some of my volunteer leadership positions. I am so appreciative that I was not; in fact, all of the organizations I was active in before the crash asked me to stay on in the same positions. I will forever be grateful for this affirmation of the value I brought. For instance, I was the CFO for the local Girls on the Run program in my area of California. After the accident, I wondered how I could be a role model, since I

couldn't walk, let alone run. But the board kept me in the position, and I went on to encourage girls to focus on what they wanted and go after it. I shared my philosophy: A great attitude can help you accomplish anything. Besides, I thought my new condition would provide a model of how to deal with adversity. I taught the girls that "it's not the adversity that defines you, but how you respond and push through it."

GOTR Fun Run Emcee

I appreciated, however, that my ability to push through my challenges as a paraplegic was easier for me than for a lot of paraplegics because I already had developed a rigorous discipline of physical activity in life before the accident. And we had the financial means to acquire a few of the things (like our motor home) that made our lives easier.

I also believe that in every bad situation, there is something good, and I am adamant about looking for it. At a minimum, I find that I can learn from the challenge or mistake and do it better the next time. And, the next time, I can focus on the best way to do something—it's amazing what can be accomplished. There's a Bible verse about this that I have always loved found in Matthew 21:22: "If you believe, you will receive whatever you ask in prayer." I know that my will to keep persevering in my adaptive sports and other rehabilitation efforts comes from my belief that God does not give me challenges that are beyond my strength or wisdom, as well as from my commitment to push through adversity.

I believe that the success in my healing, in life, and in business is because of my positive attitude. I laugh when I think about a time in my early college life when I was trying to get off work for an outside event I needed to attend. I couldn't find anyone to cover for me, so I called in sick; I was stuck between two "must-do's." Well, the day came for the event, and I ended up sick and couldn't go anyway. My lesson: I was so uneasy with my lie that I became sick!

I jokingly refer to myself now as a "retread." After a pause in my work in real estate, I have come back to a part-time role in management and mentoring at my office and also leadership roles with the local association of Realtors and the California Association of Realtors. With the passion of making a difference in people's lives, both work and the association leadership are so rewarding. The president and all positions of the local association of Realtors are volunteer positions, in keeping with my desire to give back to the real estate community.

When I first considered the volunteer positions, I was concerned that there were many long meetings to attend, and sitting in my chair would be painful. (Remember, sitting enhances the pain in my nerve-damaged legs.) Luckily, a friend in a wheelchair, Larry Spiteri, immediately visited me and convinced me that I could do it. I might sit twelve hours in a day, but I am contributing to our business and protecting homeownership rights. The energy of the leadership inspires me, and I get to see this encouraging friend at some of the meetings.

Besides, as we all know, sometimes an intense focus can distract us from chronic pain.

Teaching a class in the APR office

My day-to-day efforts in the office also inspire me. It is so energizing to discuss with real estate agents how they can specifically increase their business. After we make a plan, they usually ask me to hold them accountable. Then they take the dialogues that I have given them and practice with me, spend the time actually doing the prospecting, and come back with more business. I also love going out with an agent to meet clients face-to-face and help them earn the listing or solve a transactional problem. Sometimes, the encouragement is as simple as offering a class about the basics of contracts and how to use them. It's a special thrill when people whom I have coached become superb Realtors.

Although the conditions of my life have changed, I find that I am still the strong-willed individual that my life lessons from childhood, my college experiences, my marriage to Steve, raising my children, and holding leadership positions in the work world have made me. I am so honored that I still have the opportunity to encourage others.

Recently, a fellow paraplegic called me to express her fear and sadness that she wasn't able to do what another paraplegic could do. She was comparing herself. I so understood what she was feeling and reminded her, "No matter who you are, there is always someone better than you and someone worse than you." As I explained to her, "Focus on what you want and don't worry about what others think. Find that silver lining and enjoy all of the things that you *can* do. Your positive attitude will pull you through."

Ultimately, what I have learned is that, although we all have challenges in our lives and adversities to deal with, they don't define us if we don't let them. My accident really brought into focus what is important in life. Other kinds of life changes—such as divorces, moves, new jobs, and illnesses—can also remind us of what is really important. Bad things do happen in each of our lives, but how we react, deal with them, and find the positive is what matters.

Supporting the Los Gatos Holiday Parade

No matter what we have to deal with in our lives, we have the strength to deal with it if we believe in ourselves and give it our best effort. I regained my inner strength shortly after the accident, despite my physical condition. It's the human quality that we call resilience. I CAN STILL DO IT!

Endorsements

Captioating Journey

Karen is uniquely gifted with determination and grace, to not just live but to thrive and to inspire all those around her. Now her story will bring hope and inspiration to the thousands that read her captivating journey following a life-changing plane crash.

~ **Mark Keirstead**, Co-Founder and Executive Director of One Step Closer Therapeutic Riding

An Inspiration in My Life

Karen's return to our patrol team has truly been an inspiration in my life. After two decades of professional ski patrolling I have seldom witnessed the courage and strength that she brings to the mountain every time she puts on her cross. From the summit of Mt. Pluto to greeting our guests at mid mountain, she embodies the true spirit of what it means to be a patroller.

~ **Forrest Philpot**, Northstar California Ski Patrol Director

Creating Happy Memories Is a Choice.

Karen Trolan's personal story of courage, resilience, and patience will resonate with anyone who has come up against seemingly unsur-mountable challenges and wondered "Can I go on"? The answer is a resounding Yes. With love, gratitude, and faith, Karen shows that every experience is an opportunity to learn and that creating happy memories is a choice. Inspiring.

~ **Leslie Appleton-Young**, C.A.R. Senior Economist

Life Is What You Make of It.

Absolutely amazing, Karen's story from the accident to where she is today is truly inspiring. Every challenge that was thrown her way has been overshadowed by her accomplishments. Her dedication to family and God proves to all of us that LIFE is what you make of it.

~ **Vince Arthur**, Director of Base Area Operations, Heavenly Mountain Resort

A Horrifying Crash... Amazing Lady!

Karen Trolan is a fighter, survivor, teacher and friend. After a horrifying crash she continues to define courage and passion and has the ability to change people's lives with her will power and love. Amazing lady!

~ **Jeff Barnett,** VP & REGIONAL MANAGER, Alain Pinel Realtors®, Los Gatos, CA, CAR Director for Life, NAR Hall of Fame, Realtor® of the Year 1998 & 2008

Inspirational Journey of Hope and Grit

For close to 20 years I have had the privilege of knowing and working with Karen Trolan in the crazy world of California real estate. Compared to the rest of us mere mortals, Karen is a nova that never dims – she has always done more in less time (and generally with more heart) than anyone I have ever known.

Karen's love for skiing and flying led to a horrific accident that could have destroyed her life; however, it only served to strengthen her resolve to be the best wife, mother, REALTOR® and ultimately the best person that any of us could ever hope to be. The determination and love in the Trolan family is a wonder to behold. Karen's book is an inspirational journey of hope and grit – like Karen it stands as a testament to everyone that we should never give up on our dreams simply because of a nightmare. I CAN STILL DO IT! is a must read for anyone who needs a role model to guide them along a difficult life path.

~ **Victoria B. Naidorf**, J.D., Broker Risk Management

Double Down on Determination

By nature, people are pessimistic, even in the most optimistic of positions. I have never known anyone with more grit and enthusiasm for life than Karen. Her disabling circumstances have only pushed her to double down on her determination to succeed at everything she desires to do. Her authentic insights will richly bless those who read her story.

~ **Mike Hulme**, President of Alain Pinel Realtors

Courage and Tenacity

Karen is tenacious and has an amazing human spirit. She has worked through her challenges and prevailed. She is the same positive and active person I have known for nearly forty years. Observing Karen on a personal level after the accident, I saw this was not an easy process, yet she fought through the pain and all the medical setbacks. If you desire inspiration and need encouragement to get through the day, this is the book for you. Let Karen's journey help you improve your life and show you how to be active while living life to its fullest. She is inspirational to all of us at any level, proving the human spirit is stronger than the physical.

Every time I talk to Karen I am inspired and empowered. Her courage and tenacity are contagious. Her book will improve your life no matter your situation. **~ Holly Vargas**

Encourages Us All

A brave friend and student, Martial Artist Karen Trolan was a pilot of a small plane and in a plane crash. Her horrific injuries included paraplegia, but she had faith and never gave up hope. Her inspiring story encourages us all that we can do it. The author addresses the determination, stamina, courage and compassion of oneself facing a life-threatening condition. A definite read.

~ Samuel Kwok, Grandmaster Wing Chun, Qi Gong, Instructor, Author of TRADITIONAL WOODEN DUMMY and MASTERING WING CHUN

Persistence and Grit

When I first worked with Karen on horseback in an arena at a therapeutic riding center after her accident, I pointed to a trail high on a hill and said "If you work hard at this, we'll be riding up there someday." She and her husband now own horses of their own, plus a truck and trailer, and they camp and ride on many such trails in beautiful parks throughout California. Persistence and grit. Karen personifies both.

~ Niki Lamb

Failure Is Not an Option

A story of triumph out of tragedy. One woman's incredible story of overcoming personal injury to rise victorious. This is a must-read book when failure is not an option. Her story is inspiring.

~ Dr. Marc Stoner, Master in Martial Arts

Never Giving Up

Yep, it's a great story about life and passion and never giving up. Inspirational. **~ Shihanke Russ Rhodes**, 10th Degree Black Belt (head of system), Martial Arts Instructor, plus four other Black Belts

A Warrior, an Inspiration, and a Hero

Karen Trolan is one of the most amazing women I have ever met. She is a warrior, an inspiration, and a hero. By reading her book we can all learn about overcoming the impossible, through faith and endurance. I love this woman for who she is and what she has accomplished. Her book, I CAN STILL DO IT! is an inspirational must-read.

~ **Cynthia Rothrock**, Action Film Star (55 credits) and Producer (7 credits), Martial Arts Instructor (5 Black Belts), Inducted into the Black Belt Hall of Fame, Inside Kung-Fu Hall of Fame, and the International Sports Hall of Fame

Recommending this Book to Every Patient

Inspirational!!! This book shows the power of faith, determination, and the importance of taking personal accountability for one's decisions in how to live his/her life. I'm recommending this book to every patient of mine and anyone who has encountered a setback and wants to turn it into a comeback!

~ **Dr. James Lu**, PT, DPT, LAc, Dipl. OM, OCS, MTC, CSAS

If There's a Will, There's a Way.

This is an amazing story of a beautiful young woman who was tragically disabled in a plane crash. Her injuries have taken the use of her legs. For most of us, we would be devastated with being confined to activities sitting in a wheelchair. But this is the story of an incredible woman whom I've had the honor and pleasure of meeting because of her love for the martial arts. That's right—martial arts—and that's just the beginning. Try water skiing, snow skiing, snorkeling, and countless other activities that even people with full use of all their limbs have a hard time with. But Karen masters them easily; it's her determination and her never-give-up spirit. As a martial arts instructor for over 30 years, I've never seen anyone like her. When she found out that I taught Tango dancing, jokingly I asked her if she'd like to learn. She looked me straight in the eye and said, "Get me out of this chair; let's dance," and she had her first tango lesson. This book is an incredibly inspiring story of a never-give-up spirit that lives in all of us. I suggest you read this wonderful book.

~ **Grandmaster Mark Thomas Gerry**, eight-time Martial Arts Hall of Famer, West Coast Grand Champion, Master Instructor to the Stars, Action film and TV actor, director and producer.